KIYO SATO

From a WWII Japanese Internment Camp to a Life of Service

CONNIE GOLDSMITH

WITH KIYO SATO

TWENTY-FIRST CENTURY BOOKS / MINNEAPOLIS

I dedicate this book to all the Issei and Nisei who were unlawfully incarcerated during World War II and yet who still managed to live their lives with grace and tolerance—for the sake of the children. I also offer a grateful thank-you to Domenica Di Piazza, my longtime editor who helped bring so many of my books to fruition. —CG

Young students are the people who will make a difference in our country. They are faced with so many challenges and bombarded with information, real and fake. In my lifetime, I have been taught many erroneous historical facts. Remember, the decisions you make will not only determine your future but the future of America. —KS

Twenty-First Century Books™
An imprint of Lerner Publishing Group, Inc.
241 First Avenue North
Minneapolis, MN 55401 USA

For reading levels and more information, look up this title at www.lernerbooks.com.

Main body text set in Adobe Garamond Pro.
Typeface provided by Adobe Systems.

Library of Congress Cataloging-in-Publication Data

Names: Goldsmith, Connie, 1945– author.
Title: Kiyo Sato : from a WWII Japanese internment camp to a life of service / Connie Goldsmith.
Other titles: From a WWII Japanese internment camp to a life of service
Description: Minneapolis : Twenty-First Century Books, [2020] | Includes bibliographical references and index. | Audience: Ages 13–19 | Audience: Grades 10–12 | Summary: "This is the story of Kiyo Sato and her family and their experience in the U.S. Japanese Internment Camps during WWII."— Provided by publisher.
Identifiers: LCCN 2019046594 (print) | LCCN 2019046595 (ebook) | ISBN 9781541559011 (library binding) | ISBN 9781728401584 (ebook)
Subjects: LCSH: Sato, Kiyo, 1923—-Juvenile literature. | Satō family—Juvenile literature. | Japanese Americans—California—Sacramento—Biography—Juvenile literature. | Japanese Americans—Evacuation and relocation, 1942–1945—Juvenile literature. | Poston Relocation Center (Ariz.)—History—Juvenile literature. | World War, 1939–1945—Concentration camps—Arizona—Poston—Juvenile literature. | United States Air Force Nurse Corps—Biography—Juvenile literature. | Nurses—California—Sacramento—Biography—Juvenile literature. | Sacramento (Calif.)—Biography—Juvenile literature.
Classification: LCC D769.8.A6 G65 2020 (print) | LCC D769.8.A6 (ebook) | DDC 940.53/1779172092 [B]—dc23

LC record available at https://lccn.loc.gov/2019046594
LC ebook record available at https://lccn.loc.gov/2019046595

Manufactured in the United States of America
1-46287-46271-12/26/2019

CONTENTS

Foreword 4

1 The Last Night 8

2 An Ordinary Family 11

3 "A Scary Chill" 25

4 Tarpaper Shacks and Horse Stalls 36

5 Incarcerated in Poston 50

6 Leaving Poston 62

7 Rebuilding a Life 76

8 Captain Kiyo Sato 86

9 Kiyo's Calling 97

Author's Note 113
The Sato Family 114
Timeline 115
Glossary 117
Source Notes 119
Selected Bibliography 126
Further Information 127
Index 132

FOREWORD

After Japan bombed the US naval base at Pearl Harbor, Hawaii, in December 1941, the United States officially entered World War II (1939–1945). The US government sent people of Japanese ancestry who were living on the West Coast of the United States to incarceration camps. These people had committed no crimes. Our grandparents Shinji and Tomomi Sato were shipped to the barren camp at Poston, Arizona. They were Issei, a Japanese-language term for first-generation Japanese immigrants to the United States. Under US law, Issei were prohibited from becoming American citizens even though they had lived and worked in California for decades. Their children are Nisei, a Japanese-language term for second-generation Japanese people who were born in the United States and are therefore US citizens. Our grandparents and eight of their nine children—Kiyo, Sanji, Aizo, Kozo, Kazu, Naoshi, Tomoko, and Masashi—were held as prisoners at Poston. Their oldest son, Seiji, served in the US Army.

Details of the World War II internment of Japanese American families are becoming more widely known as a tragic yet significant part of American history. Our Auntie Kiyo has taken the responsibility of ensuring that we all learn the stories and lessons of our parents' and grandparents' time in the Poston internment camp. She describes the irony for Grandpa and Grandma to have a son serving in the army while their other children were considered "the enemy"—incarcerated and stripped of the very freedoms Seiji was fighting for.

Still, their unwavering dedication to their faith and to their beloved United States of America is truly inspiring. Our parents rarely spoke of the hardships they went through during their internment, and we don't remember our grandparents ever sharing their experiences with us. Yet we third-generation Sansei know how they handled the uprooting of their lives. We understand the blatant discrimination our family faced. Even so, we also grew up hearing about the Issei organizing sports teams and social events, creating schools, promoting church activities, and growing food crops in the inhospitable Arizona desert. Most of all, we learned about the community spirit that is such a part of our lives today. The US government took away freedom, land, and businesses. But it could not strip the Japanese in America of their integrity or their drive to do what was right for their children and for their country.

Today, as the children and grandchildren of the Issei, we enjoy a life free from the worst of the discrimination our parents and grandparents endured during wartime. Lessons of the Issei and Nisei might have been forgotten if our Auntie Kiyo did not have the passion and dedication to use her talent in writing and speaking to educate us. But Auntie Kiyo did not stop there. She has given her life to sharing with as many students as possible the tragic consequences of using fear as the justification for incarcerating innocent people based on their country of origin. Auntie Kiyo is determined that this will never happen again to any group of people.

In her published memoir, *Kiyo's Story*, Auntie Kiyo shared the lesson of the "dandelion through the crack," a seemingly insignificant flower that can endure and survive in unexpected places. Her father taught her that we are like dandelion flowers, able to thrive and grow under the most difficult circumstances. The dandelion has another lesson. It's a flower of seeds, and each dandelion will let loose its seeds upon the wind. Auntie Kiyo took the seeds of her life's stories and passed them on so that other new flowers might be encouraged to root and sprout and grow. As you read her story, you may find you bloom as well. You might even be inspired to share your own unique story, with the difficulty and beauty it may hold. That's exactly what Auntie Kiyo would want for you.

—Humbly and with gratitude for all who came before us, Jodi Sato-King, the eldest of the Sato cousins and daughter of Kozo (George), on behalf of all the Sansei of the Shinji and Tomomi Sato family

DANDELION, A HAIKU

Tanpopo ya
Iku hi fumarete
Kyoh no hana

—John Shinji Sato, as recited to his daughter Kiyo,
ca. 1970

Dandelion
You've been stepped upon—for how long?
Today you bloom!

—Kiyo Sato, translation of Dandelion, a Haiku, 2019

1
THE LAST NIGHT

We lost so much in those early days,
such treasures we had to leave behind.

—*Kiyo Sato, 2018*

On her last night of freedom, nineteen-year-old Kiyo Sato looked around her family's house near Sacramento, California. On February 19, 1942, the US government had ordered that she and her family—and all other persons with one-sixteenth or more Japanese blood—must leave the West Coast for isolated American prison camps for the duration of World War II.

"How in the world would we fit everything we needed into the one suitcase we each were allowed to carry into the camp?" Kiyo wondered. "There was a houseful of stuff—sacks of rice and baskets of vegetables, the furniture, the beds, and so many books. The piano that five of us practiced our lessons on stood in a cramped corner. And what would happen to my father's farm equipment? There was his tractor, the hundreds of wooden boxes for the strawberry harvest, and all his tools. How do you tell yourself you have to forget about all that?" Yet, even with the uncertain future, Mama and Tochan (the Sato family word for "daddy") remained calm for the sake of the younger children.

"Mama wanted to be sure we were well fed for the next day's trip," Kiyo said. "She made curry stew and rice, with chunks of potatoes, carrots, and other vegetables. After supper, Mama took care of everything around the kitchen, putting things away as if she was going to fix supper the next night. But we wouldn't be here; this was our last night at home. The next morning, we'd be on a train going to who knows where."

This portrait of Kiyo (*left*) and her mother Tomomi (*right*) dates to about 1940, two years before the US government ordered Japanese Americans on the West Coast, including the Satos, into internment camps.

After dinner the smallest children scrambled into Tochan's lap. He recited his favorite Henry Wadsworth Longfellow poem, "A Psalm of Life" and told a Japanese story about the kitsune, a clever fox who dresses in a kimono and takes the form of a human being. Then Tochan took the children to the outdoor *ofuro* (a traditional Japanese wooden hot tub) for baths. After that, Tochan tucked the little ones into bed and went to the barn to finish nailing together boxes to hold the strawberries that a friend promised to pick.

Kiyo and Mama worked in the kitchen for hours. Kiyo remembers, "We didn't know where we would be going in the morning. We didn't even know if we would be fed. I made peanut butter sandwiches

Inari Ōkami, a spirit of the Shinto religion of Japan, appears with a kitsune to a warrior. This nineteenth-century woodblock print was made by famous Japanese artist Utagawa Kuniyoshi.

for everyone with Mama's homemade strawberry jam and wrapped them in waxed paper. Mama made sticky rice balls, each with a little salted plum inside, and then wrapped the rice balls in seaweed. She didn't want us to go hungry."

Kiyo and her family raised fruit, vegetables, and nuts on their farm. For the previous ten days, she and her parents had labored to bring in the ripe strawberry crop. They needed to harvest as many of the berries as possible to sell before leaving for the internment camp. Kiyo was exhausted. Mama sent her to bed, and Kiyo fell asleep worrying about what would happen to the family's house, their farm and their belongings, and their two dogs, Molly and Dicky.

The life that Kiyo knew and loved was over.

2

AN ORDINARY FAMILY

My school was just across a field. When it rained, Tochan
carried me there piggyback. I liked the sound of rain falling
on my hat as I leaned against his warm back. I was always my
father's little shadow. He took me everywhere.

—*Kiyo Sato, 2018*

In 1941 Kiyo Sato and her eight younger siblings lived with their
parents on a small farm near Sacramento, California. Kiyo had started
college that year, and her eldest brother, Seiji, would soon join the
US Army. The younger children attended school nearby, studied hard,
and worked on the farm after class and on Saturday. On Sunday they
went to church. The Satos were an ordinary American family. Until
they weren't.

Shinji and Tomomi Sato:
From Japan to California

Kiyo's father, Shinji Sato, had come to California from Japan in 1911
when he was fourteen years old. He worked at a peach orchard north
of San Francisco in the Napa Valley with other Japanese laborers.

When Shinji grew up, he wanted to find a wife. According to US law, Japanese men living in the United States could not marry American women. Shinji would look for a wife in Japan. Time was running out. In two years, the Immigration Act of 1924 would go into effect. This US law would limit immigration to the United States and banned all immigration from Asia, including Japan. Shinji could not bring a bride to the United States after that.

Like many Japanese Americans on the West Coast in the early 1940s, the Sato family raised crops on a family farm. In this photo from 1941, Kiyo is with her parents and eight siblings. *From left, front row*, Shinji (their father), Kiyo, Seiji, Sanji, Aizo, Kozo, Kazu, Naoshi, and Tomoko. Baby Masashi is in the arms of their mother, Tomomi.

A *baishakunin*—a Japanese matchmaker— arranged a marriage for Shinji. The baishakunin guaranteed that Shinji's future wife was from a good family and that she was free of illness. In 1922 he traveled by steamboat from San Francisco, California, to Tokyo, the bustling capital city of Japan. Shinji agreed to meet the young woman the baishakunin had picked for him, but he did not promise to marry her. After working for eleven years in the United States, Shinji, now twenty-four, was reluctant to marry a woman he didn't know. He liked the way American men chose their own wives.

On his way to the village where the young woman lived, Shinji stayed at an inn in Tokyo. A woman named Tomomi Watanabe was living at the same inn. She captured Shinji's attention. People said that when Tomomi was younger, she had turned down all marriage offers and that she was too old for marriage now. Tomomi immersed herself in nursing. She cared for tuberculosis patients in a hospital down the street from the inn. Shinji noticed that Tomomi rushed to the hospital each morning dressed in a crisp white apron, returning each night with wrinkles in her clothing and satisfaction on her face. She ate alone at the inn's dining room, unusual for a Japanese woman at the time.

Shinji greatly admired Tomomi's independence and confidence, so much like that of American women. He decided Tomomi was the woman he wanted for his wife. So he asked friends to tell the family of his intended future wife that he would not be coming to meet her after all. Shinji's friends agreed Tomomi would be a good wife and acted as matchmakers. Tomomi consented to

This formal portrait of Kiyo's father, Shinji Sato, was taken in Japan in 1922, the year he traveled from California to Tokyo to marry.

This photo of Kiyo's mother, Tomomi Watanabe, was taken in 1922. It is typical of Japanese pre-wedding portraits of the time.

marrying Shinji. She had heard good things about the United States, and she was ready for new adventures. Shinji had to leave Japan within a month, or he would be inducted into the Japanese army. After a quick wedding, Tomomi and Shinji Sato took a steamship from Tokyo back to San Francisco to start their new life together.

The couple returned to the Napa Valley peach orchard. Life there was very different from life in Tokyo. Tomomi learned to pick and sort and pack peaches. She adapted to living in a small hut and to using an outhouse instead of an indoor bathroom as she had at the comfortable Tokyo inn. Like Shinji, Tomomi worked hard and soon earned the respect of the other workers. Shinji had a brother in California. A few months later, Shinji and Tomomi followed that brother to Sacramento. At the time, US law forbade Issei (first-generation Japanese in the United States) from owning land. But they could legally rent land or purchase it in an American citizen's name. So Shinji and Tomomi rented 5 acres (2 ha) of land along with a run-down house, a barn, and a water pump. It wasn't much, but it was enough for a young couple in love. They decided to grow strawberries on their farm. The fruit was new to the region, but local farmers said it grew well in the region's clay soil. It was a good decision.

When Life Seemed Nearly Perfect

The Satos' first strawberry crop—and their first baby—both arrived in the spring of 1923. On the day the baby girl came, Tomomi worked in the strawberry fields until the midwife reached the house to help with the birthing. In Japan, families wanted their first child to be a boy and felt shame if it was a girl. But in the United States, there was no shame if the first child was a girl. The Satos named their newborn daughter Kiyo. Against the midwife's advice, four days after giving birth, Tomomi carried tiny Kiyo into the fields with her, nestled on a pillow inside an empty strawberry crate. Tomomi couldn't rest when berries needed picking.

As Kiyo grew, she played in the fields while her parents worked. She especially loved her Kewpie doll, a little baby doll based on popular cartoon characters of the time. Kiyo made dollhouses out of strawberry crates. Shinji proudly took his daughter everywhere with him. Kiyo's favorite place was a small grocery store whose owner, Mr. Gomez, always stooped down to talk to her. "Then he reached into the big jar on top of the tall glassed-in counter and handed me a lollipop," she remembers.

Before long, in 1924, toddler Kiyo had a big surprise. She remembers, "Suddenly, in the middle of summer, Tomomi came home with a little baby wearing a knitted white hat and wrapped up in a soft white blanket." Tomomi and Shinji called the baby boy Seiji. Then in the winter of 1926, baby boy Sanji arrived, and two years later, baby boy Aizo. "I loved every baby that came along," Kiyo says. "They were my little brothers and sisters." This love for young children endured throughout Kiyo's life.

Shinji worked for years to learn English. Mrs. McClintock, the wife of the peach orchard owner, had taken a special interest in Shinji. She gave him lessons until he could read and speak near-perfect English. The Satos spoke Japanese at home, and Shinji wanted to teach English to Kiyo before she entered first grade. After long days of hard work, Shinji read to Kiyo and her siblings from books he bought at a used bookstore. The English words came easily to Kiyo. She learned from popular stories such as *Dick and Jane*, the *Little Red Hen*, and *Hansel and Gretel*. Kiyo's mother said *Hansel and Gretel* was a bad story for children. "A little boy and a little girl push a woman into an oven to burn. It does not matter that she is a witch!"

From then on, Shinji made up his own stories for the children. Some were about Kuzu, a simple boy who always managed to solve problems. For example, what happens if you drop a grape into a hole and your hand is too big to get it out? Easy peasy. Use your chopsticks! Another story was about a carpenter who found a bag of gold and hid it under a tatami mat at home. He was so worried about the gold being stolen that he lost all joy in life, unable to focus on anything else. One day when the carpenter looked under the straw mat, the gold was gone. Furious that his worries had come true and the gold was gone, he fell asleep. The next day, he woke up to find he was once again happy, enjoying the sun's warmth and the singing of birds. Kiyo and her brothers and sisters laughed and clapped their hands in delight. They liked these stories better.

A New Home

After Shinji and Tomomi had farmed the rented land for six years, a Nisei (second-generation Japanese in the United States) friend organized a company in his name. Unlike the Issei, the Nisei were American citizens and could own land legally. The friend purchased

RAMPANT RACISM

Early in the twentieth century, about 275,000 Japanese people emigrated from their ancestral homes in Japan to the West Coast of the United States. Like other newcomers, they were looking for a better life with more economic and educational opportunities than they had in Japan. The majority of Japanese immigrants settled in California. At that time, millions of eastern and southern Europeans were immigrating to the East Coast and midwestern parts of the United States. These newcomers had risked everything for a new life in America, which they thought of as a golden land of opportunity.

When they arrived, however, many of the immigrants faced prejudice, rampant racism, and discrimination. Their cultures, languages, and physical appearance were very different from those of the Irish and German immigrants who had come before them. Japanese culture and language were especially unfamiliar, and many Americans expressed hatred toward Japanese immigrants. For example, in 1900 San Francisco mayor James D. Phelan claimed that Japanese people "are not the stuff of which American citizens can be made."

He warned of what many Americans referred to at the time as the "yellow peril"—a racist phrase reflecting the fear that Japanese were dangerous because they were, Phelan said, "capable of taking the place of the White man." During his successful run for the US Senate in 1919, Phelan touted the openly racist campaign slogan, "Keep America White"—and won.

a large piece of land in Sacramento. Kiyo's father, his brother, and the friend shared ownership under the company name. Of that land, 20 acres (8 ha) belonged to Shinji. "Flat land extended to the horizon . . . interrupted only by a dry unattended almond orchard," Kiyo said. "On our new twenty-acre parcel, a creek ran through the middle, creating a

Until the bombing of Pearl Harbor, Kiyo experienced little of this prejudice and discrimination directly because most of her neighbors were Japanese. The white people with whom she came in contact were kind to her. After the bombing, however, everything changed.

A member of the Hollywood Protective Association points to anti-Japanese signs on her house. The association was formed in Hollywood, California, in the 1920s as part of an effort to ensure segregation and white dominance in Hollywood neighborhoods. "Japs" is a racist term for Japanese people. This photo dates to the early 1920s.

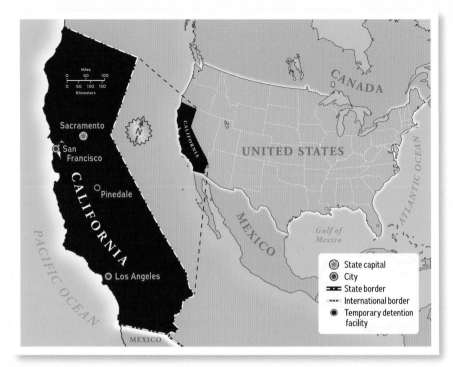

Kiyo grew up on a farm near Sacramento, the state capital, in Northern California.

deep swale [dip in the land]. Tall cattails grew where water settled."

Shinji planned to dig a well, build an irrigation system, and construct a barn where the family would live until there was enough time and money to build a house. He promised it wouldn't take long. The sound of Tomomi and Shinji hammering away at the new house after working hard in the fields all day lulled Kiyo to sleep in the barn each night.

When the new house was finished, Kiyo's brothers shared a large room. Kiyo had her own bedroom. She loved it. "Sun shone into my little room and two orange crates held my sweater and underwear. My small red diary and pencil went on top. I liked the smell of the new lumber and the clean walls and floor." The bathroom had a sink and a chamber pot to use as a toilet at night. It was more convenient than using the outhouse in the yard. An indoor toilet would come later.

Kiyo attended Edward Kelley School 2.5 miles (4 km) away. She and her siblings didn't mind walking to school each day, not even in winter. When they got to school, the teacher, Miss Mary Aline Cox, had a warm fire going in the big black stove. Miss Cox taught a large class of nearly sixty children in the one-room schoolhouse. She taught them from first grade until they graduated from eighth grade. "She was the best teacher I ever had and influenced my life for the better," Kiyo says. "She saw the talents and needs of each child. She was a taskmaster with teaching the basics: reading, writing, and arithmetic. We learned to speak in front of people and to perform on stage. I often tutored the younger children. Miss Cox was proud that every child she launched into junior high was well prepared. The school was the epitome of what a good school should be." Kiyo's close connection to her teacher would last many years.

The Sato family continued to grow. In all, Shinji and Tomomi had nine children—six boys and three girls. As the eldest, Kiyo was often responsible for the younger children because Tomomi was busy all day cooking, cleaning, sewing, and working in the fields. The children did a good job of finishing their chores, and Kiyo made sure they got to school on time. "Seiji found the puddles in the road more fun than school! I was like Mama's little administrative assistant," Kiyo jokes.

Berries and More Berries

The Satos were one of many Japanese farm families on the West Coast. Half the people of Japanese ancestry in this part of the United States—California, Oregon, and Washington—worked in agriculture. The Sato family and other Japanese farmers achieved spectacular success on poor land throughout much of California. For example, they planted strawberries between rows of grapes and irrigated both crops at the same time, increasing the yield of both. Along with strawberries, Shinji experimented with new types of berries such as loganberries, boysenberries, and raspberries. He planted grapes, walnuts, tomatoes, cabbage, carrots, potatoes, radishes, and cucumbers. The family always had plenty of fresh fruit and vegetables to add to the rice they purchased at a nearby store.

Kiyo remembers that one year a shipper ordered two crates of Shinji's raspberries to send to Canada where the king and queen of Britain were visiting. The Sato family picked the biggest and reddest berries for them. Tomomi placed a cluster of bright green leaves inside each crate as decoration because she wanted the berries to look as good as they tasted. "Several days later, another order arrived for two more crates." Kiyo said. "We knew then that the king and queen liked our raspberries."

Like the Satos, this Japanese American family in California raised strawberries and other food crops for a living. During the 1940s, before internment, Japanese American farmers were producing about 35 percent of California's fresh produce and most of its strawberries. American photographer Dorothea Lange took this photo in 1942.

From 1929 to 1942, Americans struggled through the hard economic times of the Great Depression. Millions of people lost their jobs and homes and had difficulty finding enough food for their families. But Kiyo and her family lived on a successful farm in a warm climate with plenty to eat. The Depression was hard for her to understand. "In the newspaper, we saw pictures of long lines of people waiting to get food," Kiyo said. "People were starving everywhere. I was nine years old [in 1932] and I couldn't understand . . . people waiting in line for a loaf of bread. I wondered why children didn't get enough to eat when we had tomatoes, cucumbers, and all sorts of food growing . . . in our garden."

Dreams Come True

Music and education were as important as food and books to Shinji and Tomomi. One Saturday, Shinji brought a used piano home in a friend's pickup truck. Kiyo and four of her brothers took lessons from Marjorie Fairbairn, a respected piano teacher in the area. The lessons cost seventy-five cents an hour, money well-spent, Shinji said. Kiyo also learned to play the violin. The family joined the nearby Baptist church. They attended services every Sunday and occasionally during the week as well.

Kiyo graduated from Edward Kelley School in 1938. She was valedictorian of her class of eight students. Then she entered Kit Carson Junior High in Sacramento 12 miles (19 km) away. Buses weren't available to take Kiyo to her new school, so Shinji bought her a 1932 Studebaker for $450 and gave her driving lessons. "I was convinced that I would not be able to [learn to] drive the Studebaker to town," she said. Finally, Kiyo was able to work the gears, brakes, and clutch. With her parents' permission, she got her driver's license at fifteen. As her siblings graduated from the eighth grade, Kiyo would take them to the junior high school. And when she was eighteen, she would drive to Sacramento and begin college at Sacramento Junior College, where she planned to study journalism.

Meanwhile, the family farm flourished with some of the best strawberries in the state, along with persimmons, pomegranates, almonds and walnuts, peaches, and more. Hired workers helped the Satos at the height of harvesttime each year. Kiyo ordered new school clothes for herself and her siblings from the Sears and Montgomery Ward catalogs. Life was good. It seemed that Tomomi and Shinji's dreams had come true.

Sunday, December 7, 1941

December 7, 1941, was just another Sunday for the Sato family. On this Sunday, they went to church in the morning as usual and did chores when they returned. "I remember that day so clearly," Kiyo says. "We were busy clearing the walnut orchard of branches that we'd pruned. We piled them up and lit a bonfire. Everybody helped, even my youngest brother, three-year-old Masashi. At noon all eleven of us sat down at the kitchen table; meals were always happy times for us." Kiyo spent much of that afternoon ironing her siblings' school clothes for the week. She made stew and rice for dinner, while Tomomi and Shinji finished their work in the walnut orchard. Shinji ended the day with his usual story time. "It was a perfectly peaceful family day," Kiyo says.

THE FIRST DAY OF INFAMY

World War II had begun in Europe with the German invasion of Poland in September 1939. France and the United Kingdom—known as the Allies—quickly declared war on Germany. Italy and Japan sided with Germany and together were known as the Axis powers. Seeking dominance in Asia and the Pacific region, Japan invaded French Indochina (Vietnam, Laos, and Cambodia) in 1940 and Burma (Myanmar) in 1941. The United States initially remained neutral in the global conflict.

On Monday, December 8, 1941, the day after Japan bombed Pearl Harbor, US president Franklin D. Roosevelt spoke to a joint session of Congress. The speech was broadcast live on American radio, drawing a huge audience. In the speech, Roosevelt said, "Yesterday, December 7th, 1941—a date which will live in infamy—the United States of America was suddenly and deliberately attacked by naval and air forces of the Empire of Japan." He reported the Japanese had also torpedoed US naval ships between Honolulu, Hawaii, and San Francisco. Within hours, Japanese forces attacked other sites in the Pacific, including those in the British colonies of Malaya (later called Malaysia), Hong Kong, and Singapore as well as the US possessions of Guam, Wake Island, and the Philippines.

Meanwhile, halfway across the Pacific Ocean, Japan had bombed the US naval base at Pearl Harbor, Hawaii, in a surprise attack. (Hawaii was an American territory and did not become a state until 1959.) The first wave of Japanese bombers hit Pearl Harbor at 9:53 a.m. Pacific time, just about when Kiyo got home from church. A second wave of bombers attacked Pearl Harbor at 10:54 a.m. Pacific time, when Kiyo and her family were working in their orchard.

Radios around the country reported the attack. The Satos had an old, unreliable radio. "Even if it had been working that day, we were so busy we didn't think to turn it on," Kiyo says. In an era before

Roosevelt's final words in his famous Day of Infamy speech were, "I ask that the Congress declare that since the unprovoked and dastardly attack by Japan on Sunday, December 7th, 1941, a state of war has existed between the United States and the Japanese Empire."
It took less than an hour for the US House of Representatives and the US Senate to declare war against Japan. Japan's allies, Germany and Italy, soon declared war on the United States. Britain had already declared war on Japan nine hours earlier after Japan attacked its colonies in the Pacific. With Roosevelt's declaration of war against Japan, US participation in World War II was officially underway.

Radio stations across the nation broadcast President Roosevelt's Day of Infamy speech live on December 8, 1941.

This color-tinted photo from 1941 shows the USS *West Virginia* in flames. Japanese bombers sank the ship, and others, as part of the surprise attack on Pearl Harbor on December 7, 1941.

television and computers, the family had no way of knowing that Japan had attacked the United States. Kiyo had no way of knowing that the world and her own life had changed forever. When she returned to college in Sacramento the next day, she knew immediately that something was terribly wrong.

3

"A SCARY CHILL"

Way into the night I heard the rhythmic tap-tap of Tochan's
hammer as he built boxes to hold the strawberry crop.
A Caucasian neighbor had promised to harvest the berries
and to watch over our farm while we were gone.

—Kiyo Sato, 2018

Anti-Japanese sentiment in the United States burst into flame after Japan bombed Pearl Harbor. The next day, on Monday morning, December 8, 1941, Kiyo drove her Studebaker to college, as usual. She parked in the student lot, as usual. She entered the building for her first class, as usual. But nothing else was "as usual" after that.

An Unwelcome Stranger

"I sensed that something terribly wrong had happened over the weekend," Kiyo said. "Walking down the main hallway to my class at Sacramento Junior College, I noticed that there was not the usual 'Hi, Kiyo.' Like the parting of the Red Sea, students turned their backs and walked to the side, leaving me the wide, dingy hallway. The lonely walk down the old corridor seemed interminable."

Most of Kiyo's Caucasian friends totally ignored her. Elizabeth, one of her best friends, always pestered Kiyo to copy her homework. "She didn't ask to see my homework that day." Kiyo said. "Instead, she walked right past me, ignoring me with her nose in the air. I was totally humiliated." Carol and Margaret didn't speak to her, either. Kiyo couldn't understand why most of the students she knew treated her like an unwelcome stranger, as if she'd done something bad and everyone knew about it except her. "I held my head up high and tried to be brave. I tried to shut off my feelings. Even though it seemed like everyone suddenly hated me, I kept on walking."

During a break between classes, Kiyo found a fellow Nisei student and talked with her. The girl was surprised that Kiyo didn't know what had happened the day before. When the girl told her about Pearl Harbor, Kiyo didn't understand at first why it was so important. After all, Japan was a foreign country, so why would Japan's actions make people dislike her? As a cluster of Nisei students gathered in the courtyard to talk about the attack, Kiyo began to understand what it might mean to her and her family. "A scary chill shot through my body," she remembers.

Some of the Nisei students talked about quitting school. "I was taken aback that anyone would even consider quitting," Kiyo said. Students talked of rumors they had heard of putting all the Japanese living in the United States into prison camps. "The gravity of the situation hit me," Kiyo said. "I understood the looks of hate from my classmates. Wherever I went, I felt the daggers of hate—in looks, in newspapers and at school," Kiyo said about the following days. "It was as if we dropped the bomb on Pearl Harbor, and it gave license to every *hakujin*, every Caucasian person, to spew out hatred, the worse the better."

Kiyo remembers, "We were scared wherever we went. It seemed as if there were only two safe places for us. The first was the Mills Station grocery store where the owner, John Studarus, and his assistant John

After the bombing of Pearl Harbor, the US government quickly decided to intern Japanese Americans, who, they falsely believed, could be spies and traitors. Families had only a few days to figure out what to do with family businesses and homes. Many, such as this business owner, sold what they could at deep discounts, while others arranged for non-Japanese neighbors and friends to care for their belongings until they could return.

Beskeen treated us like they treated everyone, kindly and fairly. The other safe place was Edward Kelley School, where Miss Cox protected her students like a feisty mother hen."

Because of the hatred they faced, Kiyo and other Nisei students dreaded going to school. But they wanted to continue their education as long as possible. Shinji and Tomomi supported Kiyo's decision to keep going to her classes. Kiyo sat with other Nisei students at lunch. But every day, fewer and fewer of them showed up. Many quietly quit school to escape the hatred and to help their parents on family farms and in family stores.

With the US declaration of war, Kiyo's oldest brother, Seiji, quit high school and signed up for the US Army. He was only seventeen, too young to join without parental permission, which Shinji agreed to give. Shinji was proud of his son enlisting to prove he was a good citizen. Tomomi didn't feel the same. She thought it was too dangerous. It was one of the few times Kiyo ever saw Tomomi cry, and the tears worried her.

"Our Little Japanese Friends"

By late January 1942, fear of Japanese people in the United States quickly turned into hysteria. Newspapers and politicians claimed that Japanese Americans were sending secret radio signals to Japanese submarines lurking off the California coast, that Japanese people were plotting to poison the public's water and food supplies, and that they had conspired to blow up American dams and bridges. These same sources claimed that irrigation ditches on Japanese farms were actually routes for bombers to find their way to vital American targets. Author Jerry Stanley wrote about a fire near Seattle, Washington, "It was reported that Japanese in the hills near Seattle had ignited a 'flaming arrow' pointing toward the city to guide bombers to that target." However, US Forest Service workers burning brush had actually set the fire.

These vicious, false rumors inflamed panic and paranoia. Well-known California newspapers such as the *San Francisco Examiner* and the *Los Angeles Times* printed racist tirades. For example, an editorial in the *Los Angeles Times* on February 19, 1942, said, "Since Dec. 7 there has existed an obvious menace to the safety of this region in the presence of potential saboteurs and fifth columnists [secret organization of traitors] close to oil refineries and storage tanks, airplane factories, Army posts [and] Navy facilities."

During a radio speech on February 5, 1942, Los Angeles mayor Fletcher Bowron said, "Right here, in our own city are those who may spring to action at an appointed time in accordance with a pre-arranged plan, wherein each of our little Japanese friends will know his part in the event of any attempted invasion or air raid." Even Theodor Seuss Geisel—known as Dr. Seuss—drew racist cartoons that were published in newspapers across the nation.

Kiyo's parents, like many fearful Japanese families, tried to

Dr. Seuss, who went on to great fame as an author and illustrator of humorous books for children, expressed racist anti-Japanese sentiments in his wartime cartoons. In this one—published in *PM* in 1942—he suggests that the Japanese living on the West Coast of the United States were enthusiastic members of a fifth column (secret organization of traitors).

distance themselves from their former homeland. People burned their grandmothers' precious kimonos and broke delicate porcelain tea sets. They burned photographs of their Japanese relatives or tore them up and dumped them into outhouse pits. They burned books and letters written in Japanese. They destroyed their grandfathers' ceremonial Samurai warrior swords. The US government required the Japanese to turn in potential weapons of sabotage. Kiyo's family surrendered their camera, flashlight, radio, and a rifle they used to shoot rabbits on their farm.

In January 1942, the US government announced a curfew and travel ban for the Japanese population on the West Coast. This meant that Kiyo couldn't leave home until six in the morning and she had to be home by eight at night. She couldn't travel more than 5 miles (8 km) from her house. Kiyo wondered how many people would lose their jobs, and how she and other Nisei could continue their education if they couldn't drive to school.

Kiyo remembers, "I didn't experience overt hatred when I went into town to buy food and clothing. Most of our Japanese neighbors stayed home, the safest place to be. We didn't visit each other as much as before. My parents were pretty brave to allow me to do the necessary errands. They depended on me to do those things and I know now that it took a lot of trust and courage to allow me to go out in that climate. Most of my Nisei friends were stuck at home."

An FBI Visit

Shortly after Pearl Harbor, agents of the Federal Bureau of Investigation seized more than one thousand Issei, who had lived in the United States for many years. Many of these arrests focused on people who taught the Japanese language to other Americans. FBI agents also arrested members of Japanese clubs and people with known connections to Japan. FBI raids on ordinary Japanese households increased during February 1942.

When Kiyo got home from school on February 17, 1942, a black car she didn't recognize was parked in the yard. She knew it must be the FBI. The agency had visited farms in the area and arrested many people, usually a family's father. Kiyo wondered where Shinji was and what would happen to her family if the FBI took him into custody. Kiyo felt sick with worry. She wondered, "Will Shinji be dragged away like Mr. Saiki [a neighbor], in his dirty working clothes with no time to say goodbye?"

Kiyo remembered that "my hands trembled as I pulled open the screen door. Mama sat stiff and straight, with the children crowded beside her, quiet and fearful." Heavy footsteps thudded overhead in the attic. Kiyo watched one of the three agents in his dark suit and hat as he opened each drawer in her parents' bedroom and dumped the contents on the bed. He looked under the mattress and checked the closet.

"Tochan wa doko?" (Where is Tochan?), Kiyo asked. Tomomi whispered that he was working in the fields. Kiyo prayed that he would

not come home. She feared that he would be arrested for no reason. "All sorts of things were going on in my mind," Kiyo said. "My father had his farm clothes and his muddy irrigation boots on and I didn't want him arrested wearing those. I was prepared to throw his Sunday shoes in the agents' car so he didn't have to wear those boots all the time if he went to jail."

Kiyo watched another hat-topped FBI agent rummage through her bedroom. He sat at her desk and opened all the drawers. To Kiyo's horror, he found her little red diary. Not wanting him to read her private thoughts, she said, "I stood up, ready to rush in and grab it away from him, but something stopped me. He read it, and slowly, flipping one agonizing page after the other, while I squirmed in misery." In the diary, the agent read that Kiyo and her family belonged to a Baptist church and that Kiyo taught Sunday school there. The FBI was far more likely to arrest Buddhists than Christians because Buddhism is one of the main religions in Japan. Kiyo believes that because her family was Christian, the FBI chose not to question Shinji.

The three agents finally left. "As the last agent passed Mama sitting by the door, he patted her head. 'Good Christian family,' he told her, like she'd been a good little girl."

Final Days of Freedom

Kiyo turned nineteen on May 8, 1942. A few days later, she discovered government notices nailed to fence posts and telephone poles along the dirt road leading to her farm. The Satos and other Japanese families in the area had ten days to get ready to leave their homes. They were then to report to a Civil Control Station at the railroad station in the nearby village of Perkins for evacuation to an unnamed location. Kiyo was shocked to read that each person could only take what they could carry: one suitcase apiece and bedding for the family.

Notices like this went up all over California, Oregon, and

Washington. In western coastal cities, such as San Francisco, the government gave people only six days to prepare for evacuation. Families tried to store their possessions—often in their churches— or to sell them. One man sold a new tractor for $75 that he'd only recently purchased for $750. Others sold their homes, farms, tools,

EXECUTIVE ORDERS 9066 AND 9102: THE SECOND DAYS OF INFAMY

On February 19, 1942, ten weeks after the Pearl Harbor bombing, President Roosevelt issued and signed Executive Order 9066. The order authorized the US secretary of war to designate areas of the United States as military zones from which persons could be excluded. The order did not specify Japanese Americans, but the Exclusion Zone included the western parts of California, Oregon, and Washington, and the southern part of Arizona. Ninety-five percent of all Japanese Americans lived in these places.

Some of Roosevelt's highest-ranking military advisers believed the Japanese posed a real threat to the nation's security. Congress urged evacuation and internment. And while Roosevelt himself did not fully support the move, he accepted the advice of those nearest him. For example, Roosevelt's secretary of war, Henry L. Stimson, said, "Their racial characteristics are such that we cannot understand or trust even the citizen Japanese."

Executive Order 9066 paved the way for interning Japanese Americans, and one month later, on March 18, 1942, Roosevelt issued and signed another order, Executive Order 9102. This order created the War Relocation Authority, the government agency that built and operated the Japanese internment camps.

Families of Japanese ancestry had not broken any laws. They had not been accused of or found guilty of any crime. Of the nearly 120,000 men, women, and children incarcerated in prison camps, two-thirds of them—like Kiyo and her siblings—had been born in and household goods for next to nothing: $5 for a new washing machine and $10 for a refrigerator. Another man sold his truck with four new tires for $25. One woman sold her twenty-six-room hotel in San Francisco, worth tens of thousands of dollars, for $500. They had no choice—it was that or nothing.

the United States and were American citizens. Presidents have the authority to issue executive orders. However, the US Supreme Court eventually ruled that these two executive orders violated the civil rights of loyal American citizens.

The person in charge of carrying out these orders? Lieutenant General John L. DeWitt, a man known for his deep-seated distrust and dislike of all Japanese people. He fully supported both orders and held the illogical view that "the very fact that no sabotage has taken place to date is a disturbing and confirming indication that such action will be taken."

President Roosevelt signed executive order 9066 in 1942, paving the way for the internment of more than one hundred thousand Japanese Americans during the war. His wife, First Lady Eleanor Roosevelt, was deeply troubled by the decision and tried unsuccessfully to persuade her husband not to issue the order.

Kiyo would always remember the days before her family had to leave home. "During those ten days, we didn't know night from day. I don't know if Mama ever slept," Kiyo said. "Tochan and Mama worked on the farm, harvesting the strawberries to sell so they would have some money for the family. I was taking care of everything else—the house, the packing, the seven youngest children." Kiyo put in a rush order from the Montgomery Ward catalog for new clothing for her siblings. She bought used suitcases for the family, including a tiny one for little Masashi.

"But we never talked about what was really happening in front of the younger children," Kiyo said. "They thought we were going on a train trip and they were excited. There's a Japanese saying that children should not have to worry about adult problems. That's why we didn't tell them we were really going to an internment camp somewhere."

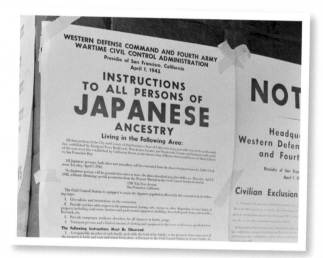

Exclusion orders in San Francisco, California, were first posted on April 1, 1942. The notices called for the removal of persons of Japanese ancestry from the city. Lieutenant General John L. DeWitt issued the orders, in this one directing evacuation by noon on April 7, 1942, less than a week from posting. The notices were specific to each city. For example, the one posted in Kiyo's neighborhood gave ten days' warning.

"Ten days passed all too quickly," Kiyo said. "The last night at home, Mama prepared a large dinner to be sure her family was well-fed for the trip to . . . where? Tochan helped the children with their baths as usual, then told them stories, with little Masashi cuddled in his lap. After the kitchen work was done, Mama cleaned up the kitchen like always, as if she would be fixing meals the next day."

Kiyo remembered, "Next, Mama and I did the laundry. We did two loads with our old wringer washing machine. It was a big job to get all the children's clothing clean and ready to pack in the morning." The moon was nearly full as Tomomi and Kiyo shook out the little overalls, shirts, and underwear and pegged them to the laundry line with wooden clothespins. The warm spring night promised dry clothing in the morning.

Kiyo was exhausted. Tomomi sent her to bed, and she fell asleep to the sound of Shinji's hammering in the barn. She knew the family must do as they were told and go where they were sent. "Years later, students asked me, 'Why didn't you riot or refuse to go?' Well, that was the worst thing we could have done," Kiyo said. "We would have been acting like the perpetrators and that was against our culture, which was to act peacefully and follow orders from authority."

4

TARPAPER SHACKS AND HORSE STALLS

We had to register and get our family number tags—one for each person and for each suitcase and bedroll. We were no longer persons, we were numbers.

—*Kiyo Sato, 2007*

The United States wasn't prepared to imprison 120,000 people for the duration of World War II. Internment camps to house them hadn't yet been built, and it would take months to do so. Meanwhile, the US government shipped people by trains or buses to temporary detention facilities, euphemistically called assembly centers. Some people were ordered to drive in family cars to the centers. These sites were hasty makeovers of fairgrounds, vacant fields, industrial sites, and racetracks. Barbed wire fences surrounded the centers, and armed soldiers stood watch over the inmates from tall guard towers.

"A Continuous Unbroken Thread"

May 29, 1942, dawned bright, clear, and warm. That day Kiyo and her family would travel to a temporary detention center until their assigned

Japanese American families arrive under military guard at the temporary detention center at Santa Anita Park, a thoroughbred racetrack near Los Angeles. Kiyo and her family were held at the Pinedale detention center near Fresno, California.

permanent camp was ready. They had no idea where it would be. Kiyo woke early in the morning to the sound of Tomomi slicing vegetables on the cutting board. "She sang a hymn, almost as if to coax the children to awaken happily. There was something about Mama, like a continuous unbroken thread that knit the family together. She got everything necessary done, like feeding and washing and loving."

As soon as Kiyo climbed out of bed, Shinji took her bedroll—her blankets and sheets—and spread them on the floor. "He placed a hammer, a large bagful of nails of all sizes, and a roll of wire in the middle. Then he rolled my blankets, covered them with rice sacking and tied the bedroll securely with the heavy rope we used to tie down loaded crates of strawberries," she recalls. As the children woke up,

Shinji took their bedrolls too. Inside each one, he hid tools and other supplies he suspected he would need to make life easier at the camp. He packed a folding saw, bucket, gallon jug, carpenter's square and plane, and bags of vegetable and flower seeds, all tucked into the folds of the bedding. He even slipped Kiyo's violin into another blanket. Kiyo feared Shinji would get into trouble if guards searched the bedrolls. She shuddered at the thought but didn't question his actions.

Tomomi ladled out rice and hot miso soup for everyone, placing sliced radishes and an egg into each bowl. Kiyo told her brothers and sisters to eat their breakfast in their pajamas and to change into their new clothes after they had eaten.

Molly and Dicky knew something was different that day. They raced around the yard at top speed, refusing to be caught. Kiyo had to tell her siblings the heartbreaking news: the dogs could not come with them. "How could I explain this terrible, cruel thing we were doing?" Kiyo remembers asking herself. "No one on this earth would miss us so much. . . . We were abandoning two members of our family." Kiyo's brothers finally corralled the dogs and shut them into a shed. Kiyo cracked the door open and propped a large rock against it so the dogs could escape later. "I turned and ran, swallowing hard to stop my welling tears as Molly and Dicky whined and scratched frantically on the shed door." Kiyo—and thousands of other families like hers—had asked local animal shelters to pick up their dogs. They found out later that no one ever came.

"Nobody Came to Save Us"

Shinji's Caucasian neighbor Bill arrived to drive the family to the train station. The men loaded all the suitcases and bedrolls into his pickup truck. Two of Kiyo's youngest siblings went with Bill in the truck. Kiyo and the rest of her family squeezed into her Studebaker and drove to Perkins. There, they continued to an elementary schoolyard where an old coal-powered passenger train waited on nearby tracks.

Caucasian workers sat at registration tables to process the hundred or so internees from the area. Behind them were soldiers armed with bayonet-fitted guns. Kiyo and her family registered with the workers, who handed each person a piece of paper with a number on it. The Sato family was number 25217. Shinji was 25217-A, Tomomi was 25217-B, Kiyo was 252175-C, and so on down the alphabet for the younger children.

"Upon orders, the guards left their posts and closed in from all directions and corralled us toward the train like a herd of cattle," Kiyo remembered. "The crowd moved peacefully, each helping the other with little children. . . . No one panicked; no one yelled." Kiyo held onto little Masashi's hand so he wouldn't get lost in the crowd.

Kiyo wondered where they were going. Did she pack enough warm clothes for cold weather, or did they need clothing for hot weather? The officials and soldiers would tell them nothing. "The train was old and filthy, like it had been parked for decades and they had brought it out just for us," Kiyo said. "Coal dust covered everything. You could hardly see out the windows; the seats were so dirty you didn't want to sit down. The boys all wore white shirts; they pulled out their shirttails to wipe off the seats where they and their families would sit."

Kiyo rubbed at a filthy window and peered out. She could see looters driving all the cars away, happy to steal from those who could no longer protect their property. Her Studebaker was nowhere in sight, no doubt stolen like so many others. As the train left the station, Kiyo caught sight of friendly faces and frantically waving hands. There on the side of the tracks were Marjorie Fairbairn, the piano teacher, and Miss Cox, the elementary school teacher, with the thirteen remaining students in Kiyo's class. They had come to say goodbye to their friends—the forty-five Nisei children on the train who had been Miss Cox's students. Kiyo waved back until her friends were out of sight. Kiyo recalls, "I kept hoping somebody would come to save us, to say that the president had changed his mind and that this was a terrible mistake. But nobody came to save us," Kiyo recalls. "Nobody. I found an empty wooden bench and sat by myself. I broke down sobbing and couldn't stop."

Cornered at Pinedale

The train lurched along for five hours. Armed guards stood at attention inside the railroad cars. "All the way, people were so supportive of one another, kind and helpful," Kiyo said. "One mother passed around sushi that she had made—seasoned rice inside a fried bean curd pocket. It made me feel better to nibble one of my favorite foods. Tomomi shared the peanut butter sandwiches with children who ran through the aisles, enjoying what was probably their first train ride. Parents stayed calm so the children could have fun as long as possible. Everything we did was *kodomo no tameni* (for the sake of the children)," Kiyo remembers. That would be a recurring theme for the next few years. Protect the children. Always.

When the train finally clanked to a stop, Kiyo looked out the window and wondered where they were. She remembered that "armed soldiers corralled an exhausted and bedraggled band of men, women, and children from the train and herded them onto waiting buses. The caravan of buses took us miles out of town into the country. The blacktop ended and we traveled along a barely visible road on flat dry terrain. Dusk lent an eerie look to the brown dust clouds churned by the buses ahead." The Sato strawberry farm seemed a million miles away.

The buses pulled to a stop late in the day. Hundreds of weary people trudged past guards and into the camp. "In the distance, in the middle of the vast dry, flat land, hundreds of black barracks enclosed by barbed wire came into view," Kiyo said. "Silhouettes of guard towers surrounded the compound. . . . At the gate, two guards armed with rifles stood. A machine gun at their feet, pointed at us, sent a chilling message."

WORDS MATTER

Sometimes people prefer to use a euphemism—a mild word substituted for a blunt but more accurate word. For example, people sometimes say that someone has passed instead of saying the person died. During World War II, the US government used euphemistic language to control public perceptions about the forced removal of Japanese American citizens to desolate camps. In 2013 the Japanese American Citizens League (JACL) published a handbook setting forth the preferred terms for events affecting Japanese Americans during that time. The league encourages use of the preferred terms.

Euphemism	Preferred term
Assembly center	**Temporary detention center** (a place where prisoners are held pending removal elsewhere)
Evacuation/relocate	**Forced removal** (the lack of choice provided to Japanese Americans ordered to leave their home)
Internment	**Incarceration** (or imprisonment, usually for a crime, although Japanese Americans had not committed crimes)
Non-aliens	**American citizens of Japanese ancestry**
Relocation center	**American concentration camp, incarceration camp, or illegal detention center** (facilities where political prisoners, prisoners of war, and minority groups are detained or confined. Kiyo herself most often uses *internment* camp and *concentration* camp.)

Authorities told the arriving passengers that they were in protective custody. But Kiyo knew it was a lie. This was a prison camp. "That moment is very clear in my memory," Kiyo says. "The camp was so crowded I feared my little brothers and sisters would get lost. I was afraid to look up at the guard towers and the young white soldiers standing at attention with machine guns. They probably had been told they were guarding dangerous spies, saboteurs, and criminals."

Kiyo soon learned they had reached a temporary detention facility called Pinedale near Fresno, California, meant to hold five thousand prisoners. The center consisted of ten blocks of barracks, each with twenty-six buildings, and living quarters for military police. Many other internees had arrived in the preceding days, filling much of the camp. A group of teen boys—also prisoners—offered to help the newcomers locate their luggage and find empty barracks for their families.

One boy led Kiyo and her family past long rows of one-room tarpaper barracks, each filled with a family. Kiyo tripped over chunks of wood that workers had left behind in the hurry of construction. She sneezed from the dust welling up around her feet. She didn't see any plants, grass, or even weeds. Everything was dry and barren. The boy went from one barracks to another, opening each door and shutting it when he found the rooms were occupied. He finally found an empty one for Kiyo and her family. "Metal cots with thin gray and white mattresses were lined up on the black asphalt floor. One light bulb hung from the rafters," Kiyo remembers.

Shinji, Tomomi, and the eight children needed ten cots. But Kiyo saw only eight in the barracks. Her brother Sanji and the other boy went to look for two more cots and to find the family's luggage. When they returned, Kiyo's siblings each chose a cot. She took one at the far end of the room. Thick layers of dust covered everything. "I caught Mama standing at the other side of the room," Kiyo said, "looking from corner to corner, lips pursed with determination, or was it to keep them from quivering?"

While the food in temporary detention centers and internment camps was adequate, it lacked many of the choices that Japanese Americans were used to eating, such as pickled vegetables and fresh fruit and vegetables. If something looked especially unappetizing, some families would take bread from the mess hall back to their barracks and make peanut butter sandwiches.

Just then she heard the ringing of the mess hall bell, announcing mealtime. Even though it was late and nearly bedtime, Kiyo and the other new arrivals needed dinner. But it was hardly worth the trek to the mess hall for a meal of stinking mutton stew, dry rice, and bread mashed with milk and raisins. "My empty stomach repelled my first spoonful of the mutton stew even before I swallowed it," Kiyo said. "I scooped the white rice, untouched by the stew, into my teacup. It tasted good." Tomomi, who normally hated to see food go to waste, barely touched her dinner.

Kiyo and her family hurried back to their barracks after dinner. "There was a 10:00 p.m. curfew. We had to get every child bathed before bed and had to brush our teeth," Kiyo said. "We had to be in our room by the curfew for the head count. *Bang! Bang! Bang!* Soldiers pounded at the door. They forced their way in, shined flashlights on everyone, and checked us off a list. I was number three. That was a little scary."

Once the family was present and accounted for, the soldiers moved on to the next barracks. "A deathly silence fell upon the camp," Kiyo said. "There were no dogs barking, no songs of summer insects or sleepy birds. No automobiles drove by. The night was warm and still. Huge searchlights scanned the compound causing weird shadows through the small windows. Each time the light hit my bed, I felt cornered and cringed inside my blanket."

LIFE IN A HORSE STALL

As part of internment, the US government prepared fifteen temporary detention centers. Twelve, including Pinedale where Kiyo and her family were held, were in California. Washington, Oregon, and Arizona each had another center. The Wartime Civil Control Administration ran the centers.

Two of the centers in California were converted racetracks. Santa Anita Park was near Los Angeles, and the Tanforan Racetrack was near San Francisco. At its peak, Tanforan held 7,816 internees, while Santa Anita held 19,000 internees. Santa Anita included about sixty horse barns, each with enough stalls to house more than one thousand horses. The US Army removed the horses just a few days before the internees arrived. They painted the stable floors and walls, but the stink of horse manure and urine remained.

Professor Yamato Ichihashi of California's Stanford University was an adult when he and his family were taken to the Santa Anita center. During his incarceration, he wrote in his diary, "A stable which houses a horse now houses from five to six humans, its ventilation is poor due to the absence of windows. A stable is generally portioned into two parts, the back part is dark. These are not only unsanitary, but mentally and morally depressive."

Actor and human rights advocate George Takei (who played Sulu

Group Showers, Group Toilets

The next day, Kiyo learned she would be showering with others in a group shower. She would have to strip naked in front of strangers, nearly unbearable for a shy teen girl. "In the shower barracks, I chose the farthest corner. . . . Showerheads protruded from the three walls, without dividers or stalls or curtains," Kiyo said. "Several Issei women squatted around cans of water, washing themselves, seemingly comfortable with their nakedness. Embarrassed, I faced the wall and awkwardly took off my clothes. . . . The women sensed my

in the original *Star Trek* television series) was five years old when he was imprisoned at Santa Anita with his family. "We were herded over to the stable area. Each family was assigned to a horse stall," he said. "For my parents, to take their three children to a crowded, smelly horse stall was a degrading, painful experience."

New arrivals at Tanforan temporary detention center near San Francisco inspect their living quarters—former horse stalls.

embarrassment and . . . kindly, they avoided looking my way, for which I was grateful."

Even worse were the group toilets inside one of the barracks. The toilet area was simply a deep trench dug into the ground. Over the trench were boards with six holes on one side and six on the other. People sat side by side and back to back to use the toilets. Mothers had to hold their children over the holes to prevent them from falling into the stinking sewage below. "The absolute lack of privacy was very traumatic," Kiyo said. "I used to hide outside the bathroom and watch people go in and come out, and when there was nobody there, I would dash for the toilets. Then I tried holding off until the middle of the night, but everybody else had the same idea."

Kiyo still has nightmares about the Pinedale toilets. "In one dream, I go looking for a bathroom and open a door to find a child's training potty that can't be flushed," she said. "In another dream, I'm walking down a long hallway, opening one door after another; each is a bathroom with a broken filthy toilet that can't be flushed. And maybe the worst one is where I'm in a luxurious mansion filled with well-dressed ladies chattering away. But I'm invisible; nobody sees me. I need a toilet and go down a hallway into a fancy bedroom. In the far corner is a little chamber pot covered in fabric. The women come in, still chatting and sipping champagne. They're having a good time, but I'm still invisible. I want to disappear. Then I wake up. Here it is, seventy-five years later and I still have bad dreams about those toilets."

"I Am Momotaro"

The internees knew their stay at Pinedale would be temporary. Even so, Shinji and others brought seeds with them. Farming was what many of them knew best. They planted a few seeds at Pinedale and saved the rest for the permanent camp to follow.

One day Kiyo spotted a group of people in front of a barracks. "I worried that somebody had died. Wherever I went, a group of children followed me. I didn't want them to see a dead person, so I led them away from the crowd." Once the children were gone, Kiyo's curiosity drew her back. "I noticed people who left that barracks looked so happy. I went over to see what was going on, and here was this bright green sprout pushing its way out of the ground. Every day I went by to look at the plant—it was a morning glory. It grew and grew, and the people took such good care of it, stringing it up against the black tarpaper and watering it." In a few weeks, the plant bloomed with bright blue flowers. This tiny bit of beauty made Kiyo happy.

Momotaro is a popular hero of Japanese folklore dating back hundreds of years and with many versions of his story. This pottery Momotaro doll was made sometime after World War II. Kiyo told his story to children in the camp.

Another time Kiyo led a group of children along the fences surrounding the camp. As they walked, she told them the Japanese story of Momotaro, a miracle baby who floats down a river inside a peach to become the son of an old man and his wife. He grows up strong and wise and leaves home to fight demons. "I am Momotaro," Kiyo told the children, "and we are on our way to slay the monster." Through the story, she was saying that the monsters were the terrible people who had put them into the camp.

"I felt like Pied Piper, gathering more and more children as we walked along," Kiyo said. She remembers that a lone fig tree grew on the other side of the fence. "I wished I could lead all the children right through the barbed wire fence to that fig tree, and let them play to their hearts' content. I would sit on that low branch and feel its green friendliness."

LASTING IMAGES

In March 1942, the War Relocation Authority hired professional photographers to record the evacuation of Japanese Americans from the western states. Among the photographers was Dorothea Lange, already famous for her photos for the Farm Security Administration that documented the Great Depression. The War Relocation Authority wanted Lange, Clem Albers, Francis Stewart, and several others to photograph the final days of Japanese Americans in their homes and farms, on their way to the temporary detention centers, and during their time in internment camps. In 1943 the government also hired Ansel Adams, famous for his outstanding landscape photos of the American West, to photograph the Manzanar internment camp.

"Dorothea was asked to photograph the evacuation of the Japanese Americans," said Elizabeth Partridge, Lange's goddaughter and author of the award-winning biography *Restless Spirit: The Life and Work of Dorothea Lange.* "The government wanted a record to show that this had been a humane process, that it had been done in an orderly way, and that there was nothing for anyone to complain about. Dorothea's feelings were very different. To her it was such a suspension of civil liberties. She wanted to make a record of what the lives were like for the people who were about to face this extraordinary event."

The War Relocation Authority told the photographers what they could capture on film. For example, photographers weren't allowed to film barbed wire or guard towers manned with soldiers and machine guns. They were told to film only what the US government viewed as positive aspects of life in internment camps. Because so many families tried to keep life as normal as possible for the sake of the children, this included ball games, parades, flower-arranging classes, sewing, and students in classrooms. Yet internees later remembered the intense heat and cold, the dust and sand that blew through poorly constructed barracks, and the breakdown of family structure. Without these realities captured on film, the photographs showed a distorted picture of internment life.

Dorothea Lange took this photograph of Japanese American and other children pledging their allegiance to the United States not long before families were evacuated to internment camps. The children were students at Raphael Weill Public School in the Little Tokyo neighborhood of San Francisco.

Even so, some of the images are as beautiful as they are haunting. Young children recite the Pledge of Allegiance in their hometown classrooms, their hands on their hearts; families pose in front of tidy homes before leaving for temporary detention centers. Some photos show farmers harvesting their last crop or children saying goodbye to their pets. Others capture city women wearing high heels and fashionably short dresses as they carry their one allotted suitcase to the train that will take them to a temporary detention center. Babies wear family identification tags as if they were pieces of luggage. Buses and trains are packed with internees. And a photo that somehow escaped government censor shows guards poised with bayonets atop a watchtower.

The seven thousand images the photographers captured are available to the public at the National Archives and the Library of Congress. They are a valuable resource for writers, historians, and others studying this part of US history.

5

INCARCERATED
IN POSTON

Maybe one must bend like the bamboo in the wind
and when the storm is over, we will be able to stand upright
again. The bamboo never breaks.

—*Kiyo Sato, 2007*

In late July 1942, Pinedale authorities announced that the permanent
camp was ready. "Just when we were beginning to feel settled,
officials told us to pack our things and be ready to leave early the next
morning," Kiyo said. "We'd only been here seven weeks. Imagine going
to all that trouble and spending all that money to put us in a temporary
shelter. My country did that to us. It's still hard for me to believe it
really happened."

Another Train Ride

"Once again the guards herded us into buses and then onto a train,"
Kiyo said. "I could tell we were headed south, away from Fresno, but
we didn't know where we were going. We talked about it and tried to

guess, but nobody knew and the guards wouldn't tell us. Authorities told us we weren't going to a concentration camp but to a relocation center for our own protection." Kiyo knew this was another lie.

Once more, Kiyo, her family, and hundreds of other Japanese American prisoners from other California towns suffered a miserable train ride to an unknown destination. The US government had chosen to establish the internment camps in isolated deserts and mountains and swamps far away from home so that internees would no longer be seen as a threat to national security. "The train was so old it must have been pulled out of mothballs," Kiyo said. "The guards told us to keep the blinds covering the train windows pulled down. The one where I was sitting wouldn't stay down and I had to hold it."

Kiyo and her family were assigned to the internment camp at Poston, Arizona. Pictured here in front of their barracks are, *back row from left to right*: Kozo, Aizo, and Tomomi (Mama). *Front row left to right*: Shinji (Tochan), Kazu, Naoshi, Tomoko, and Masashi. Kiyo's oldest brother, Seiji, took the photo when he visited Poston while on leave from the US Army.

When Kiyo's arm got tired, she accidentally let the shade snap back up. "A guard pointed his bayonet at me and told me to keep that shade down." The guards didn't say why the windows had to stay covered, but Kiyo suspected it was because they didn't want anyone outside to see who was on the train. The official message was that all

Japanese Americans were potential criminals and spies, loyal to Japan. None of them were, and most of the people on the train were women and children.

Finally, Kiyo managed to get her window shade to stay down. "I rubbed my stiffened elbow and carefully lowered my exhausted body onto the wooden bench. I rested my head on the armrest of the two-passenger seat and fell asleep from sheer exhaustion." A sudden jolt woke Kiyo when the train stopped. She peeked around the edge of the blind and saw hundreds of soldiers standing along the length of the train. Behind them, lines of curious Caucasian onlookers stared. Kiyo wondered, "What would happen if we opened our shades and waved to them and they saw all the children?" The train soon started up again, heading east. Kiyo's brothers and sisters napped; even Tomomi dozed fitfully.

"Bathed in Moonlight"

The passing scenery—viewed through the side slit of her window shade—took Kiyo's breath away. "Giant saguaros [cactuses] passed before my eyes. Bathed in moonlight, they stood like silent sentinels as far as I could see. I leaned back against the seat and dreamed, 'Someday I'm coming back here to see the whole place as a free person.'" The train skirted the southern edge of the Mojave Desert. By car on a modern highway, the trip from Barstow, California, where Kiyo's train had stopped briefly, to Poston, Arizona, takes about three and one-half hours. Kiyo's trip—in an ancient train spewing nauseating smoke into the coaches—took more than twelve.

Over time, Kiyo noticed the guards had relaxed; some stretched out in the aisle asleep with their rifles leaning against the wall. Several of the young Nisei men got up and headed toward the back of the train. Kiyo followed them, wondering where they were going. She stepped over one napping guard and then another. When she reached the baggage car, she realized she was the only female among the young

Nisei. "All these guys lounged against the bedrolls, talking with one another. I grew up with six brothers so I always got along well with men. I sat down and listened to them. I asked where we were going. One guy guessed Arizona. It turned out he was right. I fell asleep leaning against a soft bedroll as I listened to their chatter."

When Kiyo woke up, she was hot and sweaty. The train slowed down and jerked to a stop. "We were all eager to get out after so long," Kiyo said. "When the big freight door opened, there were hundreds of army trucks waiting out there in the sand. Nothing but sand and soldiers." Kiyo's family was at the opposite end of the long train. She jumped out of the baggage car and tried to run to the front of the train to rejoin her family. An armed guard blocked her way and motioned her toward the trucks with his rifle.

People stood jammed together in the truck. Kiyo could hardly see anything because the trucks churned up so much dust. "When we arrived at the camp, about 17 miles [27 km] from where the train stopped, I felt hot, dizzy, and woozy," Kiyo said. "I couldn't sit down so I just held on to the side of the truck. I got more and more dizzy. Images of Mama and Tochan flashed through my mind. When the truck stopped and we climbed out, I felt myself falling, fainting. The last thing I remembered was someone grabbing me by the elbow."

Roastin', Toastin', and Dustin'

When Kiyo woke up, she saw a huge gray slab of concrete looming inches above her head. She thought she had died and wondered if this was a morgue, a place for dead bodies. But Kiyo was not in a morgue. She was in a laundry room under a large sink, and the concrete slab was the bottom of that sink. Other people lay nearby on dozens of cots around the room.

One of the Nisei helpers realized Kiyo was awake and asked for her name and family number. "Panic-stricken, I tried to remember the five-digit family number we were all issued, knowing that finding my family depended on it. '27 . . . 21 . . . I think there's a 6,' I fumbled desperately." The man said he would help Kiyo find her family. As he led her down the aisles of people on cots, Kiyo's little sister Kazu jumped up and joined them. She had become ill on the train too but was feeling better.

The man found the Sato name in the papers he carried on a clipboard. "He took my sister and me in a Jeep, to the south end of the camp. Everywhere I looked, all I could see was desert, dirt, and sagebrush. He told me we were at Poston in Arizona and that it was nearly 130°F [54°C]." Kiyo looked for people she knew as the Jeep made its way through the camp. Crowds of children ran through the dry dirt, and adults held cloths across their faces to protect against the blowing sand. The Jeep passed rows and rows of identical shabby barracks. Thousands of people had already arrived and settled in.

Kiyo noticed that barbed wire did not separate the barracks from the desert as it had at Pinedale. Why bother? Nobody could escape across the vast expanse of dusty desolation. Poston was the second largest of the internment camps and contained three separate units. The internees called them Roastin', Toastin', and Dustin', referring to the site's extreme heat and dust. The Satos were in Toastin'. Kiyo's official address was Block 229, Barracks 11, apartments A and B, Poston Camp II.

As the Jeep crossed a road along the southern edge of the camp, Kiyo saw people bent over a large pile of straw, stuffing it into long white bags. She spotted her mother dragging one of the bags, which seemed three times her size, across the road. Kiyo yelled for the driver to stop, and she and Kazu ran to help Tomomi. "*Yokatta ne*" (that's good), Tomomi said with relief when she saw her two daughters. Kiyo picked up the other end of the heavy bag—which Tomomi told her was to be a mattress—and together she and her mother hauled it toward the family's barracks. "Mama explained that each family with six members or less got one room." So Kiyo's family qualified for two rooms.

Like Kiyo and her family, these internees at Poston filled mattresses with straw for their bedding. The beds were extremely uncomfortable, but families had no other materials to work with.

Inside the barracks, Kiyo saw five canvas cots covered with the straw-filled mattresses crowded against the wall of each small room. "Who decided we should have straw mattresses?" she wondered. "I couldn't stand it. Within minutes you're itching, sweating, and the straws poked through the mattress and stuck into your back. We rolled the straw mattress off each cot and took the cot outside and wet it from a nearby water faucet. It was cooler and more comfortable to sleep on the wet canvas than on straw mattresses."

At least the bathrooms were better than at Pinedale. They had real flush toilets at Poston instead of trenches dug into the earth. People used large empty cardboard boxes to build partitions between the toilets. Inside the Satos' barracks, Shinji nailed shelves next to the cots and then hammered more nails into the walls to hang clothes and towels. This made the cramped rooms seem more like home.

JAPANESE INTERNMENT CAMPS

During the war, the US government established a large network of sixty-nine camps and detention sites of various kinds around the country. An estimated 120,000 people of Japanese ancestry lived in one or more of these camps for at least part of World War II. These camps included the following:

- **Temporary detention centers.** Seventeen temporary detention centers were in Arizona, California, Oregon, and Washington. The Sato family was held at the Pinedale temporary detention center near Fresno. Actor George Takei and his family were held at Santa Anita Park.
- **Incarceration camps.** Of the ten incarceration camps, eight were in the West and two in Arkansas. The Sato family was in Poston, Arizona. George Takei's family was at Rohwer, Arkansas.
- **Temporary detention stations.** The FBI arrested more than fifty-five hundred Japanese nationals—Issei—whom the government considered potentially dangerous and held them without formal charges at one of seven temporary detention camps in four states.
- **Department of Justice internment camps.** These camps received the fifty-five hundred Issei from the temporary detention stations and held them awaiting their appearance before the Alien Enemy Hearing Board. The board would determine where to send them. Many were held in US Army internment camps. The prisoners weren't allowed legal counsel.

- **Citizen Isolation Centers.** In late 1942, military police at the Manzanar internment camp killed two inmates and injured many more in response to a series of violent inmate uprisings at the camp. The War Relocation Authority decided to move the men they believed to be responsible for the uprisings to isolated camps. The two remote isolation camps were at Moab, Utah (forty-nine prisoners), and Leupp, Arizona (eighty prisoners).

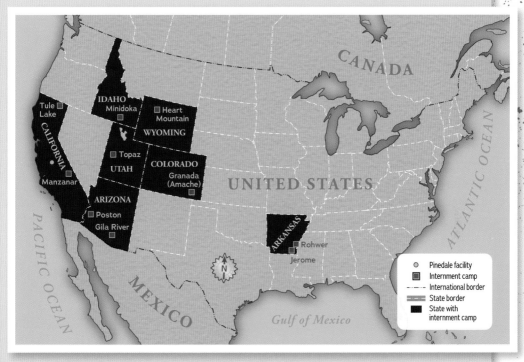

This map shows the location of the ten incarceration camps where some 120,000 people of Japanese ancestry were held during the war years.

But home was neither comfortable nor safe for Kiyo and the other internees. The camp's water came from wells dug deep into the desert and tasted as if it had come through a sewer pipe, Kiyo remembers. The wells often ran dry, and if that happened while Kiyo was showering, she had no way to rinse off soap or shampoo. Sand blew into the barracks through gaps in the walls and up through the floorboards. A layer of grit coated everything, and no amount of scrubbing could keep the dust away. Some days dust storms blotted out the sun.

Dangerous scorpions scurried beneath the cracked floorboards of the barracks. Boys killed rattlesnakes and made wallets and belts from their skins. Bands of coyotes howled eerily at the edge of camp at night. They often padded into the camp itself after dark and poked around outside the barracks and the mess hall looking for food. The coyotes scared Kiyo at first. "When I heard them, I froze and didn't dare go to the bathroom or go to get water to cool off my cot." Kiyo learned that the animals don't attack people, and she eventually got over her fear of them.

She also learned that nights could be beautiful in spite of the coyotes. Kiyo wanted to sleep outside under the stars, but Shinji didn't allow it at first. He insisted the entire family remain together at all times. "Once he relented, my brothers and sisters lined up our cots outside our barracks and slept outside under the stars," Kiyo said. "How beautiful they were. Looking at the stars gave us joy and set us free for a few moments. You felt like you were in the middle of the sky with stars all around you. We watched the stars until we fell asleep."

A Small City

With as many as eighteen thousand inmates at any given time, Poston was a small city. The government left the day-to-day business of the camp to the prisoners. The internees elected block managers to handle problems within a group of barracks. Council members organized

Ansel Adams took this photo of a baseball game at the Manzanar internment camp at the foot of the Sierra Nevada. The camp was not far from Death Valley, California, one of the hottest places on Earth. To prevent despair, prisoners tried to maintain a semblance of everyday life at the camps.

activities, such as sporting and social events. Any elected leader had to be a US citizen—a Nisei. Kiyo's father was Issei and therefore could not serve in an elected position. Instead, he became a council member adviser. The director of the camp greatly valued Shinji's English-and-Japanese language skills. He often called on Kiyo's father to translate between internees who spoke only Japanese and other people in the camp who spoke only English.

To help fill the long hours, Kiyo's father and other internees planted the seeds they had carefully hidden away in their suitcases. They planted them around the barracks and irrigated them frequently with cans of water carried from the few available spigots so the seedlings—zinnias, morning glories, radishes, cabbage, lettuce, tomatoes, cucumbers, and carrots—wouldn't dry out in the heat.

"A PRISONER IN MY OWN COUNTRY"

Kiyo had strong feelings about her experience during the war. She disagreed with the ways in which the US government described what was happening to her and to other Japanese Americans. "Our camp, they tell us, is now to be called a 'relocation center' and not a 'concentration camp.' We are internees, not prisoners. Here's the truth: I am now a non-alien, stripped of my constitutional rights," Kiyo said. "I am a prisoner in a concentration camp in my own country. I sleep on a canvas cot under which is a suitcase with my life's belongings: a change of clothes, underwear, a notebook and pencil. Why?"

Kiyo also wanted something to do. At first, she helped in the mess hall, but she really wanted to work with children. "Kids followed me around wherever I went," Kiyo remembers. "They liked me because I talked to them. When I heard the camp was starting a preschool program, I knew that's what I wanted to do." She found the barracks where one of the internee women was setting up a schoolroom for three- to five-year-old children in the camp. She had a few school supplies, a little table, and one bare light bulb hanging from the ceiling. Kiyo jumped at the chance to help. The woman asked Kiyo to tell the parents in her block to bring their young children to class on Monday.

The US government paid internees who worked in the camps a small salary. In camp schools, government rules said only college graduates could be teachers. Because Kiyo didn't have her college degree, she became a preschool attendant. "I was elated, not only to have a job but to have some spending money," she said. Kiyo received $12 per month, and teachers made $19 per month. By comparison, while an internee teacher at Poston made $228 per year, a teacher in a city school outside the camp could make $2,600 a year.

People often used their money to order items from the Sears catalog. Some bought curtains to hang in their windows for privacy. Kiyo used her first paycheck to buy new toothbrushes for her family. She also ordered feminine hygiene supplies for herself. She was tired of making sanitary pads from strips of cotton diapers, which she had to wash out by hand every night during her period.

Back on the Farm . . .

Each camp had regular mail delivery, and two months after arriving at Poston, Kiyo's father received a letter from a realtor in Sacramento. The realtor offered to buy 10 acres (4 ha) of the family's farmland for $175 per acre. Shinji didn't want to sell. But the realtor threatened to seize the land under government regulations that allowed citizens to claim land for emergency wartime use. If the realtor did this, Shinji would receive no money at all. So he agreed to sell this piece of his land at the unfairly discounted price, although it was worth much more. After the sale, Kiyo's family still owned another 10 acres. However, many Japanese families lost their houses, farms, and businesses—everything they had worked so hard for—because they couldn't pay rent, mortgages, or taxes while incarcerated.

Soon after, a bill from the electric company in Sacramento arrived. Shinji had no way to pay the bill and realized that someone must be living in the family's house and using electricity there. He wondered how long he and his family would be at Poston. Months? Years? And would they have a home to go back to at all?

6
LEAVING POSTON

I looked up at the limitless sky, filled with the most brilliant
stars . . . the same stars I would see from our farm
in Sacramento. Is there anyone . . . who was trying to
get us out of here? Or did they plan for us to shrivel up
in this desert and just quietly disappear?

—Kiyo Sato, 2007

By the fall of 1942, government authorities and other leaders began
to question the wisdom of holding tens of thousands of able-bodied
citizens in internment camps. For example, American leaders such as
War Department official John J. McCloy began to push the Roosevelt
administration to allow Nisei to serve in combat. In February 1943,
Roosevelt announced the creation of a segregated battalion composed
of Nisei soldiers commanded by white officers. The battalion would
serve in Europe to help meet the need for more soldiers. It would also
serve as a propaganda weapon to counter Japanese claims of American
racism. In stark contrast to Roosevelt's Executive Order 9066, which
sent 120,000 people of Japanese ancestry to internment camps,
Roosevelt said about his decision, "No loyal citizen of the United States

should be denied the democratic right to exercise the responsibilities of his citizenship, regardless of his ancestry."

"I'm Free!"

Educators and government leaders, such as university presidents and Milton Eisenhower (the first director of the War Relocation Authority and brother of future president Dwight Eisenhower), began to advocate for students to be released from the internment camps to attend colleges outside the Exclusion Zone. Religious organizations such as the Quakers pointed out that internment unnecessarily deprived young people such as Kiyo of an education. Kiyo's father worked with the camp administrative office, so he knew just about everything that happened both inside and outside the camp. Shinji heard the US government had set up programs to encourage colleges in the Midwest and on the East Coast to accept interned Nisei students. He urged Kiyo to apply. In July she wrote to the War Relocation Authority asking for a release to go to college. Kiyo couldn't choose where she wanted to go—a college would have to select her. August passed, then September, without a response. Kiyo gave up hope of returning to school.

One morning in early October 1942, the camp postal carrier handed Kiyo an official-looking letter. She ripped it open. She read the letter once. Twice. It granted her admission to Hillsdale College, a Baptist college near Lansing, Michigan. "I'm getting out. I'm free!" she screamed, waving the letter over her head. Children came running, worried that a scorpion had bitten Kiyo. She didn't know much about Michigan, but returning to college thrilled her.

"I was going back into that world that sent me to a concentration camp," she said. "I didn't know exactly what would happen. A Baptist organization funded my tuition, room, and board in one of the college dormitories for the first year. I was the first student in my camp block to be released," Kiyo said. "I was going to see the world again. Imagine that!"

"*Yokatta ne*" (that's good), Tomomi said in her restrained manner.

Kiyo was one of forty-three hundred Nisei students released from internment camps in 1942 to attend college. Some of the older women internees at Poston criticized the decision, saying to Kiyo, "'Your parents are sending you out there to the people who are responsible for bringing you here? How can they do that? Now you're going to go out and face that hatred.' I was fortunate because my father encouraged me to leave; he made me feel confident about going on with my education. He would have done the same thing—forge ahead with confidence, not fear."

Before Kiyo left Poston, the camp director's wife took her into town for a suitcase and new brown-and-white saddle shoes. The camp social worker gave Kiyo some clothes she had collected for her. Kiyo left Poston with one dress, two blouses, two skirts, a sweater, socks, underwear, pajamas, a red jacket, and a brown purse. All fit neatly into her new cardboard suitcase.

Kiyo took a train from Poston to Chicago, Illinois. Catherine Embree, one of the Caucasian teachers at Poston, had asked her parents, who lived in Chicago, to let Kiyo stay with them overnight. Kiyo looked around the train station and recognized the Embrees from Catherine's description. They took Kiyo to their house. Their kindness made Kiyo feel safe. "As we sat at the dinner table, thoughts of home welled up." Homesickness surged through Kiyo. She wondered how long it would be before her family could sit at their own table on their farm again.

Catherine's mother took Kiyo into her daughter's room and opened the closet. She invited Kiyo to pick out some clothing for herself. Kiyo selected a dusky blue cotton dress and a brown velvet suit. "I was so grateful for the nice clothes; I loved that dress and wore it forever. The suit was more formal, but I wore it a long time as well." The next morning, after a tour of Dr. Embree's office at the University of Chicago where he taught, the Embrees put Kiyo on the train headed to Hillsdale.

TWENTY MINUTES TO REMEMBER

The train Kiyo took from Chicago on her way to Hillsdale made one short stop in Elkhart, Illinois. There, a young blond baggage porter approached her and said hello. He asked Kiyo where she was from. Kiyo didn't need any help with her luggage, so she nodded politely and kept walking. He trailed after her and asked her to have a cup of coffee with him at the lunch counter inside the train station.

Kiyo agreed. "He was curious, not prejudiced," she said many years later. "He kept asking me questions. He'd never seen an Asian face before. It was the first time I ever talked about Poston. He was interested and sincere, and I answered all his questions honestly. It felt good to be able to talk about it. He had never heard about the camps and was absorbing everything I said. Telling the boy about the camps paved the way for me to talk to all the groups I've spoken to over the years. That's one of the interesting things in life. You can meet someone for twenty minutes and it can have a lifelong impact." Kiyo later tried to find the young man to thank him, but because she didn't have his full name, she was never able to locate him.

Kiyo at College

Kiyo started college four weeks after the school year began. She enrolled in sociology, psychology, religion, English literature, and Spanish. These classes were prerequisites for her ultimate goal of a degree in science. She also remembers a class called the Geography of South America, taught by a professor who had voted against her acceptance at Hillsdale. "I enrolled in the class to prove to the professor that I was a loyal American. Would he fail me because he hates 'Japs' [an offensive term for Japanese people]?" she wondered. He did not.

Kiyo got a job working in the campus library and at the dormitory telephone switchboard, where she connected callers to the people to whom they wanted to speak. She earned thirty-five cents an hour, which wouldn't be enough to pay for a trip back to Poston over the upcoming Christmas break. Kiyo had always been with her family over the holidays. The thought of being apart nearly broke her heart.

The campus would close for several weeks over Christmas break, so Kiyo had to find a place to live during that time. The Nicholsons, a couple from nearby Garrett, Indiana, invited Kiyo to stay with them. Their daughter Goldie had visited Kiyo's church in Sacramento for a

LETTERS TO MISS COX

In 2009 Kiyo Sato spoke at the Smithsonian National Museum in Washington, DC, about her internment experience. After the presentation, archivist David Haberstitch asked Kiyo to stop by his office. "He put me in a climate-controlled cubbyhole, gave me white gloves, and brought in a tray holding a folder. In that folder were letters I'd written to my favorite teacher, Miss Cox, along with letters that my brother and our cousin had also sent her. Although I never met him, the military intelligence agent assigned to investigate me when I requested a release to go to college had later traveled all the way to Edward Kelley School in Sacramento and confiscated the letters we'd written to Miss Cox. Imagine that!"

This photo of Mary Aline Cox, Kiyo's favorite teacher, was taken in Sacramento in the late 1930s. Kiyo remembers that Miss Cox was very fashionable and always wore a hat.

month before the war, and they knew of her family. When Kiyo arrived at the Nicholson home, Mrs. Nicholson gave Kiyo a room with lace curtains overlooking snow-covered trees. Kiyo was sure Shinji would have composed a haiku about the beauty outside her window. "The thought burst a dam I'd held together . . . all these weeks, and my sobs and tears flowed uncontrollably," she said. "I tried to muffle them so my hosts wouldn't hear me downstairs. I cried until there were no more tears left."

This is a letter that Kiyo wrote from Hillsdale College to Miss Mary Aline Cox on December 26, 1942:

Garrett, Indiana
Dec. 26, 1942

Dear Miss Cox,

I often think of you and the Edward Kelley School. I hope you are well. Has the school changed? I wish I can be back there.

I am having my vacation in Garrett at the Nicholson's, and what a change it is from the dormitory life! It took a lot of studying to catch on up on the three weeks that I had missed. So far I haven't made a "C" anyway and I'm glad of that. But the trouble is that I've got only one "A" and that in Spanish. The rest were all "B"! I'm trying my best to do better.

I am taking sociology, psychology, religion, English literature, and Spanish. My reading speed is a great handicap in all my courses. I am trying very to increase my speed by timing and reading easy material as fast as I can. I can't understand how I was able to read so many books in grammar school. It takes me hours and hours to digest a chapter in sociology.

I really enjoy staying in a dormitory because it gives me so much time to study. I couldn't do that at home. I spend most all my time studying. At this rate I should make nothing but "A"'s.

The students and the professors are very kind. My stay has been very pleasant. But the people in town stare at me whenever I go shopping. I hope they get used to seeing me around.

You know how much I hate to speak before people. I was asked to speak to a ladies group and I feel that I should. They don't a thing about this evacuation. They even thought that I had come from Japan. As they asked for it, I feel it would make them understand even a little if I spoke. I am surprised at myself for not refusing to talk.

At this rate it's going to take me hours to finish this letter. It's about three years since I took typing and that was for a semester. I'm trying to polish up during vacation.

It rained so much yesterday that all the snow have melted. It is good to see the green grass again. But how I miss the sunshine! The gloomy days are going to make a gloomy long-faced lady out of me. The few times that the sun did shine, it was so uplifting that I sang and hummed all through the "duration". I can hardly wait until spring. Sunny California is certainly a good place. Too much sunshine in Poston and too little in the states out here.

I really miss home and I think of it too much but home isn't home anymore. I wonder when all this will be over and when the people will be able to be in their homes in one piece

I've spent so much time on this letter, I think I'd better quit now.

Lovingly yours,
Kiyo

Shinji is doing pretty well in Fort Leonard Wood, Missouri. I'm glad he's there instead of the camp. He is an assistant boxing coach and a first class private.

Remember Makoto? He is getting along very well. He is a corporal. Teyeko is in Arkansas camp. I know she is having a hard time with 2 step-parents to take care of.

I owe much to you, Miss Cox, for my being here.

Kiyo.

"A Piece of Coal in the Snow"

In January 1943, Kiyo returned to school for classes. One day a trio of students interrupted Kiyo at the dormitory switchboard where she was working. They gathered around her with excited faces and handed her a box. Kiyo lifted the lid and peeked inside. Tissue paper covered a blue sweater and a blue-and-white wool plaid skirt. They were the first new clothes Kiyo had since leaving Sacramento. "I was overwhelmed and choked up and didn't know what to say except 'thank you.'"

Kiyo learned her fellow students had collected money to pay for the gift. Their kindness eased the sting of feeling like an outcast. Kiyo often felt alone and out of place, especially in the dining hall where most students sat with their fraternity and sorority friends. "I sat with the independents, those who could not or did not join a sorority. In the sea of white faces, I felt as conspicuous as a piece of coal in the snow," she said."

One rainy spring day, a man in a dark felt hat and an overcoat approached Kiyo on campus. She knew immediately he was an FBI agent. For nearly five hours, he grilled Kiyo about her family, especially her father. He asked the same questions repeatedly, and she gave the same answers. After the interrogation, Kiyo went to her dormitory so shaken by the experience that she could never recall the specifics of the questions, only that the agent suspected Shinji

Like Kiyo, her brother Sanji was released from Poston to go to school in Hillsdale, Michigan. This formal portrait of Sanji was taken at Hillsdale in 1943.

of being a spy. Years later, she contacted the FBI twice asking for a copy of the interview, which she knew the agent would have documented. The FBI told her no such record existed.

Weeks after the interrogation, Kiyo received a letter from the War Relocation Authority. The letter told Kiyo that she was the first internee to be released to the State of Michigan and that the future of other students in internment camps depended on her behavior. She took the responsibility very seriously.

Apparently, the FBI agent found her behavior acceptable because four other young internees from Poston soon

The US government eventually allowed some young people to leave the internment camps to continue their education. Kiyo and her brother Sanji (*center*) were released to schools in Hillsdale, Michigan. There, Kiyo accompanied Sanji to his high school prom in 1943 because the school forbade interracial dating.

arrived in Hillsdale. One of them was Kiyo's brother Sanji. He attended Hillsdale High School, and the three others attended Hillsdale College with Kiyo. Sanji lived with a Caucasian family in a big house that hosted all four Poston students. Unlike Kiyo, Sanji didn't have to pay tuition, but he still needed money. So he took whatever work he could find to help pay his expenses." He washed dishes, cleaned houses, and worked in a nursery tending the plants.

Sanji's outgoing personality made him popular with the other students. At the end of the semester, the students at Sanji's school asked him to speak at the junior prom. The parents were in an uproar. They wanted a Caucasian kid to be the prom speaker, not the Japanese boy. The kids insisted Don Sato, as he was known, would be the speaker.

Don didn't have a date and the high school wouldn't allow him to take a Caucasian girl, so he asked Kiyo to go with him. She borrowed a lacy, white cotton gown with an off-the-shoulder neckline from a friend at Hillsdale. "I was so proud of Don standing up there and doing a beautiful job of speaking. I can't remember what he talked about, but we had a really nice time when we danced."

Struggling to Keep Up

Kiyo worked hard to pay her expenses at college. But it seemed she couldn't keep up no matter how hard she tried. She worked in the library and at the switchboard. She lived with a family, took care of their children, and did their housework. She worked in a beauty shop, ironing towels and uniforms for the staff. She filled in at the college kitchen on weekends. She studied until 2 o'clock each night, and by the spring of 1944, she was working, studying, or going to school almost every hour of every day.

Kiyo had also started to speak to churches and civic groups in Hillsdale, Detroit, and surrounding areas about her internment camp experience. "I told the truth about the camps. It was all news to them, as people in that part of the country didn't know anything about the internment. I thought it was important for them to know what happened to us, how the government treated American citizens." Some people seemed shocked. Others didn't seem to understand completely what Kiyo was telling them.

Under the stress, Kiyo's grades slipped and she was so discouraged that she decided to quit school. So when a US Navy recruiter came to the Hillsdale campus, Kiyo went to sign up. She remembers that she seemed to make the young man in his navy uniform nervous. "He fumbled for words. I waited. All I wanted to do was to serve my country like my brother [Seiji]. I didn't understand why he was so agitated." The recruiter excused himself to make a phone call. When he came back, he informed Kiyo that he couldn't accept her into the navy.

She didn't bother to ask why. She knew why. At the time, only the army accepted Japanese Americans.

Kiyo decided to go home. Her brother Don handed her an envelope of money from his work at the nursery. "He told me to use the money for my travel expenses," Kiyo said. "I tried to convince him that he'd earned the money and that he should be the one to go home, but he insisted it was for me." However, home was no longer Sacramento, nor was it Poston. Her family was living in Colorado. It had been two years since she'd seen them, and it felt like an eternity.

Colorado

With so many Americans in the military, the war had created a shortage of farmworkers. Without enough people to harvest crops, they could rot in fields across the country. The US government began to offer leave to internees who could work in agriculture. So while Kiyo was away at school, Shinji had signed up to work on a 50-acre (20 ha) sugar beet farm near Keenesburg, Colorado. It was better for the family than staying in Poston, he wrote Kiyo. Her family left Poston in the spring of 1944, each with twenty-five dollars and a one-way train ticket to Colorado, paid for by the US government.

Kiyo left Hillsdale early that summer to meet her family in Colorado. She arrived in Denver

A Japanese American farmworker labors in a sugar beet field in the 1940s. Kiyo's family decided to take work on a similar farm in Colorado in 1944 when the US government offered to release them from Poston to do so. They remained in Colorado for about a year.

late in the day after a long, tiring train ride. She asked a clerk where she could catch a bus to Keenesburg, which was another 50 miles (80 km) away. But there was no bus service, and Kiyo didn't have enough money for a taxi. She sat on a bench inside the train station feeling sad and lonely and tried to think of an answer.

Finally, she remembered Takeo Toguchi, a young man she had met at Poston. He had served in the US Army, returned to Poston after his discharge, and then moved to Denver to join his family as the camps were closing. Kiyo found his number in the phone book, and Takeo answered right away. He sounded pleased to hear from Kiyo. She told him she needed advice on what to do. He said he would pick her up and take her to Keenesburg himself. "Swallowing tears of relief, I sank onto a bench. Finally I would connect with my family!"

Home Again

Kiyo and Takeo arrived at the Satos' tiny house on the beet farm about midnight. Takeo banged on the door, shouting that Kiyo was home. The family spilled out the front door in their pajamas to greet her. She remembered that "Masashi . . . pulled me by the hand, eagerly leading me into the house." The family was together again, and Takeo headed back to Denver.

As Tomomi fired up the big black stove to drive the chill from the air, Kiyo's brothers gave her a tour of the house, proudly pointing out their bunk beds. Tomomi showed Kiyo the couch where she would sleep—a bench that Shinji had made from the wood of a locust tree he'd cut down. Tomomi covered it with sheets and comforters. "I slid between Mama's fresh, sun-dried sheets and fell asleep with thoughts of moonlight shining through my window back home, the long difficult two-year journey now only a memory," Kiyo said.

Home was where her family was, and Kiyo was home again.

Kiyo woke to the happy chatter of her brothers and sisters in the kitchen. After a breakfast of pancakes and hot Ovaltine made with fresh milk, everyone big enough to work picked up a hoe and set off for the beet fields. Working with beets was far more difficult than working with strawberries! The rows of beet plants had to be thinned, and the smaller ones pulled up or cut off to give the biggest plants the best chance of survival. The two youngest children carried water and graham crackers to their parents and siblings.

At harvesttime in the fall, the family dug up the mature beets in the cool, predawn darkness. Some beets were as heavy as bowling balls. Kiyo had to spear each beet, pull it up, lop off the green leaves, and toss it into the pile of harvested beets. Shinji told stories to help the time pass. The younger kids worked quickly on their rows of beets so they could keep up with Shinji and his stories.

As fall turned into a cold and snowy winter, the school bus couldn't make its way through the snowbound dirt roads to pick up the younger children. Inside the cabin, wet laundry hung in every room to dry. Kiyo missed the eggs, green vegetables, and fresh fruit they had always had in Sacramento. Here in Colorado, Shinji stored turnips and carrots outside by burying them in the ground, and Tomomi had a few potatoes from the garden. She made big pots of stew from those vegetables and added canned corned beef, sardines, or Spam. Peanut butter and jam waited in the cupboard for emergencies. But it wasn't the same as her mother's homemade strawberry jam.

Spring arrived. Determined to finish her college degree, Kiyo enrolled in Western State Teacher's College (later renamed Western State Colorado University) in Gunnison, Colorado. "Much of the time I was on an archeology field trip. It was so interesting. We hiked along a high cliff where American Indians used to live in caves in the Four Corners area—the place where New Mexico, Arizona, Colorado, and Utah meet. Then I took my final credits through a correspondence class from the University of California at Berkeley." Hillsdale accepted the credits from both institutions and awarded Kiyo a bachelor of science degree in 1944.

Kiyo Scouts Ahead

One night the sound of Tomomi and Shinji arguing woke Kiyo from sleep. She'd never heard them argue before. Her brother Seiji was due to return from fighting on the battlefields of Europe. Tomomi wanted him to return to the family farm in Sacramento, not to a beet farm in Colorado. Shinji said they didn't have enough money to move back to California, that they needed another year on the beet farm to make enough money to start over. Tomomi felt that if they got to Sacramento, they could work on other farms for pay and grow their own vegetables again.

Tomomi and Shinji argued into the night. Kiyo wiped away her tears and finally fell asleep. She learned in the morning that her mother had won the argument. The family would return to Sacramento. Shinji thought it best for Kiyo to go ahead to check out the farm while the rest of the family stayed in Keenesburg a little longer and worked in the beet fields.

The war was not yet over, and Kiyo had to obtain government permission to take the train to California in January 1945. Her travel papers were printed on white paper, which meant she wasn't under suspicion. Yellow papers meant a person was on the government's suspect list, while gray or black papers meant a person wouldn't have been allowed to return to California at all. She remembers thinking, "Why do I need this permit? Don't they trust us, even after all these years?"

As Kiyo's train moved west, thoughts tumbled through her head. She remembered the past. "Even after almost four years, memories were raw. Like an apparition, I could see the soldiers with bayonets standing guard at both ends of my coach." She worried about the present and the future. "Was I doing the right thing going home? Was it safe? Should we have waited? Will our house still be there? I was numbly aware of the passing telephone poles and the clickety-clack of the wheels on the tracks."

When Kiyo arrived in Sacramento, she walked along a downtown street, worrying about how people would react to her. She was hungry, and she remembers, "I checked each eating place. For what, I wasn't sure. Would they serve me? Would they be friendly? Would they at least ignore me and accept my money?" Kiyo knew she was one of the first Japanese Americans to return to Sacramento. "The further uptown I walked, it became more obviously white; I knew that my chances [of getting served] were not good." Kiyo turned and walked the other way. When she saw Chinese and black faces going in and out of a place called Hart's Cafeteria, she went inside. She felt safe enough to have a lunch of meatloaf, mashed potatoes, and limp green beans.

When Kiyo finished eating, she phoned her friend, John Beskeen, who worked at the Mills Station grocery store. He had written to her while she was at Poston. He sounded happy to hear from Kiyo and offered to pick her up and take her to the farm. "As soon as I hung up the phone, all my brave defenses melted away and I wanted to sit down and cry. It was so good to know that there was someone who would risk being seen with me."

Beskeen soon arrived, and Kiyo hopped into his car with relief. He smiled at her, and they chatted about people they knew as he drove. On the way, Kiyo was shocked to see her family church had recently burned down. Wisps of smoke still drifted from the blackened remains. She noticed dead crops and dying trees on neighboring Japanese farms ruined by neglect. She hoped things would be different at her home. "My heart skipped with joy, as we turned right at our mailbox onto our farm road. There was something warm and comforting about the brown dirt with its old familiar ruts. The road was damp, as if it had rained recently. Four more power poles and I will be home!" Beskeen made the final turn, pulled up in front of the barn, and turned off the engine.

Kiyo got out of the car and looked around. She stared in surprise at cows roaming the walnut orchard. Cows? Her family had never owned cows. The cows stared back at her, equally surprised.

7

REBUILDING A LIFE

Hopeless, quiet anger welled in my chest, knowing that most of
our neighbors lost their properties and would not
be coming back, all the years of hard work gone
under orders of our president. Shattered dreams lie
mute on the eroded, barren rows.

—Kiyo Sato, 2007

Kiyo turned from the cows in the walnut orchard and started
toward the house. Everything was gone: the farm equipment, the
work truck, Shinji's tractor, and all the tools. Garbage, empty cans,
and broken car parts littered the property. The barn door hung by a
single hinge. The peach and plum trees were dead, the walnut trees
overgrown and neglected.

Kiyo told herself that her family was lucky because they at least
had something. Many internees had returned to little or nothing. They
found their businesses had been looted, their homes vandalized, and
their churches burned to the ground. Trees had died of neglect, and
fields were sprouting weeds instead of crops.

When Kiyo reached her house, she stopped for a moment in the

Like many other Japanese Americans who had been interned during the war, Kiyo and her family came back to the ruins of their family farm. This large and elegant house in central California belonged to the Hirahara family, who raised strawberries before they were interned at the Rohwer internment camp in Arkansas. The home was returned to the Hirahara family after the war and was later abandoned. It is now on the National Register of Historic Places.

yard. Half buried in overgrown weeds, the yard was cluttered with broken bottles, piles of newspapers, boxes, and broken toys. Boards and a rusty tin sheet covered the home's shattered windows. Even Tomomi's beautiful flower garden was gone. She quickly hatched a plan. She would get a job, live in the barn, and clean up the house and yard before her family arrived from Colorado.

Kiyo walked up to the house and pulled open the screen door, intending to go inside the house to see what it looked like. The sound of squabbling children reached her ears. Children? In her house? What should she do?

"I summoned my courage, straightened up, and knocked," Kiyo

remembers. "The partially open doorway filled with many little tow-headed children. 'Mommy! Somebody's here,' one yelled. A thin young woman with wisps of blonde hair falling over her harried face appeared at the door. I explained to her that my family was returning and that we would like to have them find another place to live." The woman stared speechlessly at Kiyo. "With a heavy heart, I turned and left."

Kiyo wondered how the young family had survived in the ruined house. She didn't have the heart to evict them, yet she herself had no place to go and could not send for her family.

Then she thought of Mary Aline Cox, her former teacher at Edward Kelley School. Maybe she could help. Kiyo and Beskeen drove to the Mills Station grocery store to phone Miss Cox. Without hesitation, she invited Kiyo to stay with her and her sister Sue until she found a job and a place to live.

The Cox sisters welcomed Kiyo. After dinner the sisters retired to their rooms. Alone, Kiyo remembered that "sitting in the quiet of the night, shades pulled down behind the crisp, white lace curtains, I felt safe again. One more hurdle and I would be in my own room, with the breeze wafting through my open windows, falling asleep to the symphony of the frogs down in the creek."

About a week later, a group of people knocked at the Coxes' door, asking the sisters to sign a petition to restrict that part of Sacramento to Caucasians. Meaning no Japanese. "I dared not think about what discussions the delegation had before a group volunteered to rid the area of its first Jap, me," Kiyo said. She didn't want to cause her friends any trouble, so she quickly came up with a plan.

A Temporary Solution

The first step was to get a job, and a week later, she had found work as a maid with the McDonnell family in Sacramento. Dr. McDonnell and his wife explained the job was temporary because they were waiting for their own maid to be released from an internment camp. They paid

Kiyo forty dollars a month and provided her with a room and food. "I was glad to have a job and a place to live," Kiyo said. "And I was very grateful to be getting some money."

Several weeks later, after Kiyo finished her day's work at the McDonnells one afternoon, she took a bus to the country to see her farm again. Walking the last 5 miles (8 km) to her house, she passed farms devastated by years of neglect. Kiyo knew all the families to whom the farms had belonged: the Sakumas, Toguchis, Kitadas, and Matsumotos. She felt bitter. "How could President Roosevelt have signed an order to banish us into concentration camps, 120,000 people, with no regard for their properties?" she said. "It didn't seem possible that a few years ago our farms were vigorously producing and the area was known as the Strawberry Capital of the World, shipping . . . loads of top-quality strawberries to all parts of the country."

The young family was still in the Satos' home, so Kiyo turned away from her house and cut through the fields to a neighboring farm once owned by the Abe family. Crisp white curtains hung in the windows. Clearly, someone was living there. "With trepidation, I climbed up the front stairs. My heart pumped faster. My hands became cold and clammy." Kiyo told herself she should turn around and not bother the people inside. Instead, she took a deep breath and knocked. "I stood glued, listening to the heavy footsteps of a man coming from the back of the house."

A middle-aged Caucasian man answered the door with a look of surprise. His face and voice were kind. He immediately made Kiyo feel safe and welcome. She introduced herself to him, and the man told her he was Captain Fitzgerald. He invited her into the house and said he was stationed at nearby Mather Air Force Base. Kiyo told him that her family owned the neighboring farm.

Kiyo asked Fitzgerald if he knew what had happened to her dogs. "I listened with an aching heart as he described how Molly and Dicky looked for us. 'Every day they came back and searched madly around the house and around the barn and all over your property. The next morning they came again and frantically looked all over for you. They wouldn't stop to eat or drink.' Where did they go?" Kiyo asked, holding her breath.

The dogs got thinner and weaker each day, Fitzgerald said. Even when they could barely walk, Molly and Dicky kept looking for their family. Eventually they didn't return, and Fitzgerald never saw them again. Kiyo sobbed. "Our dogs had not abandoned us," she said, "even when we were abandoned by our classmates and even by our president. We had left two helpless members of our family to fend for themselves. How many pets, I wondered, had roamed in search of their families and died of grief after our incarceration?" Molly and Dicky's suffering still haunts Kiyo.

"An Amazing Thing"

Kiyo worked for the doctor and his wife for the next three months, saving money for her family's return. The McDonnells treated her kindly, and the maid's quarters were pleasant. In the spring of 1945, Kiyo got a letter from Shinji. He and her brother Ron, as well as an adopted cat, would be driving to the farm from Keenesburg very soon. Tomomi and the rest of the children would be coming by train to Sacramento the very next day!

Kiyo panicked. Her family couldn't stay at the doctor's house. They couldn't stay at the farm. The other family was still there, and the house was a disaster. And she didn't have enough money for a hotel. What could she do? Dr. McDonnell knew of an apartment whose owner, Mr. Osada, was still in an internment camp and was willing to rent the apartment to her. The apartment had a kitchen and a long hallway with small rooms on either side. Kiyo was so grateful her family would have a roof over their heads that she didn't even ask how much the apartment cost. She discovered later that Mr. Osada charged only sixty cents per day for her entire family.

The McDonnells took Kiyo to the train station the next morning to meet her mother and siblings. Kiyo explained that a family lived in the Sato home and that Tomomi and the children would be living temporarily in the Osada apartment. "It was an amazing thing," Kiyo said. "Mama agreed that it was right to leave the woman and her little kids alone for the time being. She had a way of accepting things and we just worked around it."

The McDonnells dropped off the family at their new apartment. Kiyo and Tomomi fixed dinner from leftover food her mother had carried on the train. Kiyo put a rice ball into a cup of tea, her favorite way to eat rice balls. "How good it tasted slurping down the softened rice, retrieving the salted, red pickled plum from the center to eat in small bits. Each warm swallow comforted my stomach. We would all be together again."

One day, while working at the McDonnells, Kiyo got a phone call. It was Shinji. He had arrived in Sacramento, and he was at the Mills Station grocery store. He had been to the farm and said that the young family was still living there. With his usual kindness, Shinji agreed with Kiyo to let them be. "We all understood that family too was suffering. All these little kids and that ramshackle farmhouse with the windows boarded up. I don't know how they even cooked there because the gas tanks had been stolen."

Kiyo left work and met her father a few blocks away. She showed him where her mother, the children, and she were living. Seven-year-old David jumped up and down, shouting and waving his arms with excitement. Everyone helped to unpack Shinji's car. David coaxed the cat—which he'd named Cat—from his perch in the car's back window and carried him into the yard. The next morning, Kiyo went to work, and the younger siblings went to school. Ron attended Sacramento High School, George went to Kit Carson Junior High School, and the four youngest went to Edward Kelley School, the same schools Kiyo had attended.

Fixing the Farm

Kiyo's father returned to his farm. He didn't speak to the woman living in his house nor did she speak to him. Instead, he cleaned up the place over the next two months. He cleared out the garbage and got rid of the rats. He shoveled piles of cow manure from the barn and deposited it under the orange trees to fertilize them. He pruned walnut trees and watered bushes. He planted a new vegetable garden for Tomomi.

One morning when Shinji arrived at the farm, he realized that the young family had disappeared overnight. Kiyo and Tomomi worked for more than a week to make the house livable. "Mama and I scrubbed every wall and the floors with water and bleach to make sure it was clean enough for us to move in."

The farm was ready for Kiyo's family early in the summer of 1945. By early May of that year, Germany had surrendered and the war in Europe was over. The conflict in Asia continued, and Americans wondered when the war with Japan would come to an end.

Meanwhile, to prepare for the family's move back to the farm,

"I KNOW YOUR HOUSE"

Kiyo could have legally evicted the woman and her children when she first returned to the family farm, but she didn't have the heart to do so. "And that was the right thing to do, because you never know what's ahead," Kiyo remembers. "A few years later my brother Don was teaching in Rancho Cordova, a small city outside Sacramento, and got to talking about his childhood. He told the students that his family had lived on a farm near Mather Air Field. One of Don's students said, 'Oh, I know your house'. He'd been one of those tow-headed kids living in our house. Imagine that! He had such happy memories of living on our farm. Conditions were so poor I don't know how they survived. But if I'd evicted them, that boy would have been harmed, and his brothers and sisters as well."

Tomomi stayed up late the night before moving day to make rice balls with salted plums inside, boiled eggs, chicken teriyaki, salted cabbage, peanut butter and jelly sandwiches, and a thermos of hot green tea. Graham crackers and milk rounded off the menu. On moving day, Shinji took the family's belongings from the apartment to the sparkling clean house. "It looked like evacuation day in 1942, carrying our suitcases filled with clothes," Kiyo said. "Only this time we headed home instead of to a camp." It meant joy instead of despair.

Helping Others

One evening Kiyo and Tomomi were making sandwiches for the children's school lunches. Shinji told them that the US government was closing all the internment camps, and everyone had to be out by the end of 1945. Yet thousands of people remained in the camps, those who were too old, too young, or too sick to find jobs, and those who had no homes to go back to.

Kiyo could see Shinji had something important to talk about. "I just heard the Inouyes have no place to go," he said. "With nine young children and only one able adult [Mr. Inouye was ill], no one wants them." The Inouyes had been good neighbors. Kiyo remembered that Mrs. Inouye often invited her and her younger siblings into the house for Kool-Aid and crackers on their way to school.

"What do you think, Mama?" Shinji asked. "Can we manage with nine more children here?"

Kiyo knew her parents never hesitated when it came to helping someone in need. They would find a way. Shinji fixed up a workers' cabin on the property. He paneled the walls with new lumber and built a kitchen. He extended electricity and water lines to the cabin. And he paid the higher utility bills as if both families were his own. "Mama and I scrubbed and cleaned three workers' rooms in the barn for sleeping and for storage of [the Inouyes'] baggage," Kiyo said. "With nineteen people, our farm looked like a mini-Poston camp. Only we were free!"

KOREMATSU AND ENDO: TAKING IT TO COURT

Two landmark US Supreme Court cases grappled with the incarceration of Japanese Americans during World War II.

***Korematsu v. United States* (1944).** Fred Korematsu was a twenty-three-year-old Japanese American citizen in San Leandro, California, who refused to report to the Tanforan Assembly Center with his family on May 9, 1942. So on May 30, the FBI arrested him. While in jail, the American Civil Liberties Union—an organization that works to defend the rights and liberties guaranteed by the US Constitution—used his case before the Ninth Circuit Court of Appeals in San Francisco to challenge the constitutionality of the government's order to incarcerate American citizens. The ACLU lost the case, and

Fred Korematsu (*third from left*) with his family in 1939

Korematsu joined his family at the Topaz incarceration camp in Utah. Meanwhile, Korematsu's attorneys appealed the decision, and the US Supreme Court agreed to hear his case. In 1944 the court upheld his conviction. In a split decision, six of the nine justices found that his detention was not based on race but on military necessity. In his dissent, Justice Robert Jackson strongly disagreed, saying, "Korematsu . . . has been convicted of an act not commonly thought a crime. It consists merely of being present in the state whereof he is a citizen, near the place where he was born, and where all his life he has lived."

Another team of attorneys reopened Korematsu's case in 1983. They had discovered that a government attorney had withheld a critical intelligence report documenting that Japanese Americans posed no military threat to the United States. In November 1983, a San Francisco federal judge overturned Korematsu's conviction, clearing his name. However, the original US Supreme Court decision still stands.

***Ex parte Mitsuye Endo v. United States* (1944).** Mitsuye Endo was a twenty-two-year-old secretary working for the State of California in 1942 when the state fired all of its Japanese American employees. Endo and her family were sent to the internment camp at Tule Lake, California, and then to the Topaz camp in Utah.

Meanwhile, the Japanese American Citizens League (JACL) sought to legally challenge the incarceration of American citizens. They identified Endo as the ideal person to represent wrongfully interned Japanese American citizens. Endo was a Methodist, had a brother in the army, spoke no Japanese, and had never been to Japan. When a JACL representative visited Endo at Tule Lake, she was initially reluctant to participate. Years later, she said, "I agreed to do it at that moment, because

Mitsuye Endo, in the office where she worked before internment at Tule Lake. This photograph dates to 1942.

[the JACL] said it's for the good of everybody, and so I said, well if that's it, I'll go ahead and do it."

It took two years of appeals for the Endo case to reach the US Supreme Court. During that time, Endo declined the government's offer for an early release from internment, choosing to remain at Topaz with her family.

The US Supreme Court did not address the question of whether her incarceration was constitutional. However, in December 1944, the justices unanimously ruled that the government could not continue to detain loyal citizens, and the government began freeing Japanese Americans. Families were allowed to go home in January 1945, and the camps were closed over the course of the rest of that year.

8
CAPTAIN KIYO SATO

My father always said he didn't care if his children were rich or famous, he only wanted us to be good citizens. I wanted to prove I was a good American, and so did my brothers.

—*Kiyo Sato, 2018*

Incarceration completely changed the direction of Kiyo's life. In 1941 she had been happily pursuing a degree in journalism in Sacramento. The next year, she and her family were in an internment camp. She lost hope of completing her education. After her release from Poston to attend Hillsdale College, Kiyo couldn't settle on a major. She tried social work, art, psychology, and microbiology, but they didn't seem right for her. She considered teaching but decided against that too. What should she do?

Kiyo loves children. She enjoys helping others. One career path—nursing—seemed to combine all of Kiyo's goals, and it would allow her dreams to come alive.

"Dean Della Rowe at Hillsdale, who had always believed in me, said I had a good academic record," Kiyo said. "She told me I should apply to three nursing schools that required a bachelor's degree. "In spring 1944,

On the left, Kiyo poses on the steps of her dormitory at nursing school in 1947. In the 1948 class photo at right, Kiyo is second from the left on the top row. She and her classmates graduated from the Frances Payne Bolton School of Nursing at Western Reserve University in Ohio.

I had applied to Yale University School of Nursing in Connecticut, Johns Hopkins School of Nursing in Maryland, and Frances Payne Bolton School of Nursing at Western Reserve University [later renamed Case Western Reserve University] in Ohio. I waited optimistically to hear back, hoping my dream would become a reality."

Three Times Rejected

But Kiyo had to postpone her dream. All three nursing schools rejected her because of her race. The United States was still at war with Japan, and many Americans looked at all people of Japanese heritage with suspicion. The letter of rejection from Johns Hopkins, dated June 6, 1944, said, "Last year our Board of Trustees advised that we should not admit to our school or employ Japanese who would have personal contact with patients."

The three rejections devastated Kiyo. "When universities of such high standing stoop to such practices, whom can we depend on?" she wondered. "How did all this happen? And how did the highest court of our country, the Supreme Court, bless our internment? What is happening to America?"

Trying Again

After returning to Sacramento in 1945, Kiyo would have been happy to help her family restore the farm. "But my parents wouldn't let me stay," she said. "They felt that it was far more important for me to finish my education. They said that was my job, not to pick peaches and pears, like I'd been doing all summer."

World War II officially ended on September 2, 1945, when the emperor of Japan surrendered to the United States. Many cities throughout Japan had suffered severe damage from Allied bombings. The United States dropped the world's first atomic bombs—one on Hiroshima on August 6 and the other on Nagasaki on August 9. About two hundred thousand civilians died in the blasts, and the two Japanese cities lay in utter ruin. Over the next few decades, many of the Japanese who had survived the atomic bombs would die from radiation sickness and cancers.

The US Air Force took this photo of the utter devastation at Nagasaki, Japan, after the atomic bombing of the city.

KEY LOCATIONS IN THE PACIFIC
DURING WWII

International border
Capital city
City
Air field/air force base

SOVIET
UNION

CHINA

HOKKAIDO

NORTH
KOREA

Sea of
Japan

HONSHU

North
Pacific
Ocean

SOUTH
KOREA

JAPAN

Hiroshima

Tachikawa
Air Field

Tokyo

Onjuku

SHIKOKU

PHILIPPINES

Nagasaki

KYUSHU

LUZON

Miles
0   80   160

0   80 160 200
Kilometers

Clark
Air Force
Base

Angeles

East
China Sea

MINDORO

SAMAR

PANAY

LEYTE

RYUKYU ISLANDS

NEGROS

Miles
0   100   200

PALAWAN

0   100 200 300
Kilometers

BORNEO

MINDANAO

Kiyo thought that with the end of the war, her chances of getting into nursing school might be better. More than anything, she wanted to live up to her parents' expectations. Kiyo knew she would feel more comfortable in the Midwest than she would on the East Coast, where Yale and Johns Hopkins are located. So she applied only to Frances Payne Bolton School of Nursing at Western Reserve University in Ohio. Kiyo was right. Western Reserve accepted her.

Kiyo moved to Ohio in the summer of 1945. It was hard to say goodbye to her family, but she was excited to be pursuing her dreams and her family's dreams for her future. While working toward her master's degree in nursing, she enrolled in the school's Cadet Nurse Corps Program. This program would prepare her for service in the military as a registered nurse. Kiyo graduated in the fall of 1948 after twenty-eight months of study. Kiyo's parents were proud of her but had expected all along that she would complete her college education. It was too far and too expensive for them to travel to Ohio for her graduation.

Kiyo worked in a local hospital for six months and then applied to the US Air Force. Like her brothers, Kiyo wanted to serve her country. The air force accepted Kiyo but didn't immediately call her to duty.

Meanwhile, Kiyo returned home. She got a job with the Sacramento County Health Department and worked for nearly two years as a home health nurse. "It was such a surprise to be accepted in my own county to work after the government put me away as a possible saboteur!" she said. "I really enjoyed public health nursing and loved listening to people's stories about their lives and families." Most of her patients were new mothers, newborn infants, and people with tuberculosis, a contagious lung disease common at the time. Kiyo worked in public health nursing from 1948 until late 1950. She returned to Western Reserve University for a semester of postgraduate work in nursing. Education was always a high priority for Kiyo and her family.

In 1950 the Sacramento branch of the Japanese American Citizens League elected Kiyo as its president. She was passionate about the organization's mission to safeguard the civil rights of Asian and Pacific Islander Americans. Her work with the JACL was one of her first forays into lifelong human rights advocacy. "I was interested in educating our younger generation because they would make decisions in the future. They needed to know what happened to the Japanese Americans during WWII. When I was with the JACL, I also worked to educate the public on our return from the internment camps. There was so much prejudice, even more than right after Japan attacked Pearl Harbor."

The Korean War

Shortly after the United States entered the Korean War (1950–1953), the US Air Force called Kiyo to active duty. American hospitals in Japan and the Philippines needed nurses. Some nurses worked in mobile army surgical hospitals (MASH units) in Korean war zones. These units were set up close to battlefields so wounded soldiers could receive immediate care. But Kiyo first received orders to report for duty at Sheppard Air Force Base (AFB) in Texas. The air force inducted her into its Nurse Corps as a first lieutenant on January 1, 1951. She would spend the first months of her wartime service stateside.

Even as a member of the US military, Kiyo faced some of the same prejudice in Texas that she had faced in civilian life. In 1948 US president Harry Truman signed Executive Order 9981, which said, "It is hereby declared to be the policy of the president that there shall be equality of treatment and opportunity for all persons in the armed services without regard to race, color, religion or national origin."

Many people noted the order did not specifically ban segregation in the military but only promised equal opportunity. Racial segregation remained legal both in and out of the military. "In the military, we were in it together for the sake of democracy; that's why I volunteered," Kiyo said. "But I was constantly reminded of another 'war front.' Black nurses and I were refused service at a Texas restaurant. It was no different than the [civilian] world."

Months later, the air force transferred Kiyo from Sheppard Air Force Base to Clark Air Force Base in the Philippines. "My most rewarding experience was a day spent with Mrs. Mariano, a public health nurse in the town of Angeles, just outside Clark AFB," Kiyo remembered. Many of Mariano's patients lived in bamboo huts built on stilts. Kiyo worked with the other nurse one day, climbing up and down ladders to reach patients. They cared for newborns, gave immunizations, and provided advice to new mothers. "That was tough," Kiyo said. "I was glad I didn't have to climb ladders every day!"

When an officer at Clark offered Kiyo the opportunity to work at the US AFB in Tachikawa, Japan, she readily accepted. Although Kiyo's parents had been born in Japan, she had never been there and looked forward to learning about her parents' homeland. Kiyo's brother George was serving with the US military in South Korea, and he could visit her in Japan when he was on leave.

In Japan Kiyo cared for American soldiers injured on Korean battlefields and evacuated to the hospital at Tachikawa. Kiyo especially relished the times she and flight nurses accompanied patients as they were transferred by plane from Korean MASH units to her hospital. Kiyo said, "I took care of men with gunshot wounds as well as orthopedic injuries. But what surprised me was that many of our patients were military dependents—the wives and children of the American soldiers living in Japan. We had a lot of pediatric and maternity patients, and I enjoyed the work. This was a good period of my life."

Shinji's Daughter

While Kiyo was in Japan, her cousin Hannah Sato visited her. They decided to explore their fathers' birthplace, Onjuku, a small city in eastern Japan. An uncle took them to meet their grandmother. "When I met my grandmother, she was very sick," Kiyo said. "She was in and out of consciousness. When my uncle woke her, he said, 'This is Shinji's daughter.' My grandmother grabbed my hand and held it so tightly that it hurt. She somehow understood that her son Shinji had made it, and that he had a good life in America. She said, 'With this I am relieved. I am ready to die.' And she died the next day. It was a very moving and emotional experience for me."

Kiyo also made time for fun. She took the train to Tokyo for shows and to see Kabuki. This form of traditional Japanese drama includes highly stylized song and dance that relies on exaggerated gestures and body movements to express emotions.

"My most memorable times were spent exploring the countryside by bicycle with my brother George. . . . He would fly down [to Tachikawa from Korea] for visits. When I signed out a car, it was my brother who was saluted at the gate because he was driving." Kiyo knew the soldiers should have saluted her. The bars on her uniform clearly indicated she was an officer and outranked her corporal brother.

Kiyo's colleagues wanted her to remain in the air force, but she had many other things she wanted to do with her life. When her two-year enlistment ended in December 1952, she left the Nurse Corps with the rank of captain, Air Force Reserve, and returned to the United States. "My time in the air force was a milestone in my life. It prepared me for the next steps in my career," Kiyo said.

The Nurse from Outer Space

Kiyo returned to Sacramento and was delighted to live on the farm with her family again. She decided to specialize in school nursing because she loved working with children. She got a job with Sacramento County, which assigned her to fifteen elementary schools. "I did what I thought was most important with the limited time I had at each school," she said. "I checked vision and hearing and made referrals to social services for children who needed extra care."

A big part of Kiyo's work was vision testing for very young children. Often those children couldn't respond correctly to image-based letter charts. "Picture charts, which showed images such as a boat, flag, star, and heart, among others, were problematic because children might call the images by different names. And the so-called tumbling E, which shows the letter E left, right, up, and down—well, some of the kids just couldn't figure that out."

The difficulties so aggravated Kiyo that she invented and copyrighted a completely new vision test in 1975. "I went home one day especially frustrated and couldn't sleep that night. I had an idea. The next time I tested vision, I added a head, tail, and beak to the E on the standard chart so that it looked like a bird. It was easy for a little kid to point with one finger to show which way the bird was flying." Kiyo's system, called the Blackbird Vision Screening System, was so successful that some schools around the country adopted it.

Kiyo also developed an ingenious way to give hearing tests to toddlers. She knew that wearing headphones frightened some children, with a nurse pushing buttons on a strange machine to send very

high- and low-pitched sounds into that child's ear. So Kiyo became the nurse from outer space.

On her head, she wore a silver-painted Styrofoam bucket with antennas (*left*). She talked to the toddlers she was testing through a toy microphone she made from silver cardboard. When Kiyo sent low-pitch

VFW NISEI POST 8985

The Veterans of Foreign Wars (VFW) is a nonprofit service organization of veterans and military service members. The VFW supports and advocates for veterans who served the United States in wars overseas. However, when Nisei soldiers returned to the United States after fighting in World War II, the VFW declined to accept them as members. So in 1947, Nisei soldiers established about a dozen VFW posts in California.

Following her return from serving in Japan during the Korean War, Kiyo became the first female member of Sacramento Nisei VFW Post 8985. As of spring 2020, she is the only surviving female Nisei member. "A primary goal of our Post is to educate the public, especially young people," Kiyo said. "We've taken our presentation, 'The Internment of Americans of Japanese Descent,' to schools for more than thirty years."

Five of Kiyo's six brothers served in the US military. Steve Seiji Sato served in the all-Nisei 442nd Infantry Regiment in Europe during World War II. This famous regiment was the most highly decorated unit for its size and length of service in the history of American warfare. Don Sanji Sato served in World War II as a translator for the US Military Intelligence Service. Like Kiyo, Ronald Aizo Sato and George Kozo signals to the kids, she told them the sound came from Santa. She said the higher pitch sounds came from Superman, C3PO, and Big Bird. The children loved to hear from their heroes through their (real) earphones connected to the (real) audiometer machine. And when the children heard the different pitches, Kiyo told them to let her know by dropping a tinfoil moon rock into the space hat she gave them. "Kids loved these hearing tests from outer space," Kiyo said. "They all eagerly participated in their hearing test, something they might not have done in a doctor's office."

Sato also served in the Korean War. Peter Naoshi Sato served stateside after the Korean War. Steve Sato and George Sato were also members of Nisei VFW Post 8985.

As a VFW member, Kiyo is frequently interviewed on radio and television on Veterans Day, and she has been grand marshal of several Veterans Day parades in California. In 2019 a veterans' organization for women selected her as the Sacramento Home Town Hero. As part of that honor, the Sacramento Kings basketball team featured Kiyo and her story on their jumbotron during halftime at one of their games.

As a veteran, Kiyo is proud of having served in the US Air Force Nurse Corps during the Korean War and often wears this hat to commemorate her service.

A Family of Her Own

Kiyo married three times although she says she doesn't usually count the first one. "I was married less than a year to a military officer. It was a mistake because I was too young. I don't even consider it a marriage."

In 1958 Kiyo married Gene Viacrucis, a talented painter in California. He too was a military man and had served in the US Navy. "By then I was thirty-five years old and wanted children," Kiyo said. "We didn't want to wait around, so Gene and I adopted four children over a ten-year period. We always asked for the next available [mixed-race] child because that was the child that needed us the most." Five-month-old Cia was the first to arrive in 1959. She was Chinese and Dutch. Two-year-old Jon came next; he was Chinese and Irish. Four-year-old Paul, of Italian, Irish, and Filipino heritage, was the third child. Cia had been begging for a baby sister, so six-month-old Tanya, of Japanese and Dutch heritage, came last.

Kiyo's husband left her in 1976 after nineteen years of marriage. "It was one of the most difficult things I ever experienced," she said. "Whenever the children were out of sight, I broke down and cried. After adopting four children, it never occurred to me that we might divorce. My children brought me great joy and heartache, and they've been my awakening. Before my father died, he told me that Gene and I couldn't have done any better with the children."

Kiyo navigated the challenging waters of single parenthood while working full-time in school nursing. She married for the third time when she was eighty. "You'd think I'd know better by then, wouldn't you?" she jokes. "Along came this man who seemed perfect. But he wasn't perfect. Nobody is." They divorced about seven years later. Kiyo remains single and active in her mid-nineties.

9

KIYO'S CALLING

Here I am all these years later, still talking about
the internments, still writing about it, still feeling that we
need to teach our young people the truth in history
because they are the ones who will make
the important decisions for our country.

—*Kiyo Sato, 2019*

K iyo retired from school nursing in 1985 when she was sixty-two years old. But she didn't retire to a quiet life at home. Instead, some of the busiest and most rewarding years of her life lay ahead. Over the past thirty-five years, Kiyo has spoken to thousands of people: college, high school, and middle grade students; book clubs; civic organizations; libraries; nursing homes; churches; and veterans groups. During a 2011 interview with the National Japanese American Historical Society, based in San Francisco, California, Kiyo said, "History is written by somebody who won the war, somebody who is a leader, somebody who was a victor. This is why all of this [speaking about the internment] is so important. We need to record our own history."

A New Direction

Kiyo has spoken to many students, but one particular high school visit galvanized her to broaden her speaking career. Kiyo's niece, Jodi Sato (Kozo George Sato's daughter), had invited Kiyo to speak to her high school history class in 1975. "We were learning about World War II," Jodi said, "and the teacher asked if any of us knew of a person who could talk about the Japanese experience. I asked Auntie Kiyo and she said yes. I was so excited about her coming to my class. Back then I was excruciatingly shy and insecure. At the time, I was one of a handful of Japanese Americans at Cordova High near Sacramento. Transitioning from a multi-ethnic neighborhood to a mostly Caucasian school was lonely. Some kids called me 'Jap' or 'slant-eyed' or mimicked talking Japanese in front of me. I felt comfortable hanging out with the African Americans. They were my friends and stood up for me. So, when Auntie Kiyo was speaking, I was proud to hear her talk about the Japanese immigration and internment experience. She did such a good job."

Jodi's classmates were interested in what Kiyo told them. "After Auntie Kiyo left, the teacher asked the class, 'Knowing what you know now, how many of you would still have the Japanese Americans interned?' I looked around the room and half the class had their hands up. I felt rejected, especially because black hands went up as well as white hands. It was then that I realized that discrimination

Jodi Sato King inspired her Aunt Kiyo to broaden her educational message to include young people.

does not discriminate. I felt more alone than ever." Even so, Jodi wouldn't change what happened that day. "I hadn't realized this experience was an impetus for Auntie Kiyo's determination to educate young people about the Japanese American experience. Thanks to her work, we've come a long way. That moment was a gift to humanity."

When Kiyo learned the results of the classroom vote, she knew she had more work to do. She went to her Nisei VFW colleagues and told them about the vote. "We agreed to organize a speakers' bureau to educate students about the internment," Kiyo said. "Twenty-five veterans agreed to participate." Even though all the Nisei speakers were volunteers, the group needed money to develop programs and to pay for materials such as a projector, large storyboard panels on easels, and photographs. "My niece Rhonda Sato (Masashi David Sato's daughter) helped us get a grant from the California Civil Liberties Public Education Fund. Even though we didn't advertise, we got busy very quickly. At our peak, we made seventy-five visits in one school year! Teachers told other teachers about our presentation. Some schools asked us back each year to speak to new students."

Rhonda Sato remembers attending some of the presentations. "The students were so interested in what Auntie Kiyo had to say. Every eye was fixed on her. There was no fidgeting or whispering. The kids got it. They understood."

What Would You Do?

For her school visits, Kiyo developed activities to help fix the internment story in the students' minds. She called one activity "What Shall I Take?" Students list what they might pack in the one suitcase they would be allowed to carry to an internment camp. The first time around, some kids included video games, phone chargers, iPads, and a mini-refrigerator. When Kiyo reminded the students those items did not yet exist, the lists of what to take became more relevant: first aid kit, sleeping bag, clothes, toothbrush and toothpaste, soap, and paper and pens.

A particularly poignant exercise was a questionnaire about internment camps that Kiyo developed and had high school students complete. "The US government is at war with your ancestral homeland and orders you and your family into an internment camp based on your race when you did nothing wrong. What would you do?"

Kiyo keeps binders with hundreds of handwritten letters from teens she has spoken to over the years. Some comments and reactions are amusing, and others are moving. The teens said:

- "I thought you were a wife of one of the veterans you were with. When my teacher said you were a captain in the Korean War, I was surprised and impressed."
- "The stories you and your friends told made me laugh at times, but I came to my senses and saw how people discriminated against you."
- "I respect how you take your time to visit schools and teach us about yourselves and your stories, which are valuable."
- "The internment was a clear violation of the Constitution and your rights. I pledge to stand up and fight if history tries to repeat itself."
- "It was very courageous of you to fight for your country even though it had betrayed you. Not only were you fighting a war, you were fighting prejudice."
- "What really bothered me was that the government took all of your possessions and never gave them back. Once I turn eighteen I plan to be very politically active and vote for as many things as I know about."

Making Amends

In 1970 the JACL began to press for reparations—payment made to make amends for a wrong—to those who had been unjustly interned in World War II. In 1979 Senator Daniel Inouye of Hawaii and several other Japanese American members of Congress proposed a commission to consider reparations. And in 1980, Congress established the nine-member Commission on Wartime Relocation and Internment of Civilians. The commission would review Executive Order 9066, the presidential order that had authorized the internment of Japanese immigrants and Japanese American citizens.

The commission heard from about 750 witnesses in ten US cities over a six-month period. Kiyo Sato was one of those witnesses. She spoke to the commission in August

THE WHITE HOUSE
WASHINGTON

A monetary sum and words alone cannot restore lost years or erase painful memories; neither can they fully convey our Nation's resolve to rectify injustice and to uphold the rights of individuals. We can never fully right the wrongs of the past. But we can take a clear stand for justice and recognize that serious injustices were done to Japanese Americans during World War II.

In enacting a law calling for restitution and offering a sincere apology, your fellow Americans have, in a very real sense, renewed their traditional commitment to the ideals of freedom, equality, and justice. You and your family have our best wishes for the future.

Sincerely,

George Bush

GEORGE BUSH
PRESIDENT OF THE UNITED STATES

Along with many other Japanese Americans who had been interned during the war, Kiyo received an official letter of apology from the president of the United States. She received hers in 1990, signed by President George H. W. Bush.

1981. "Four of us from Sacramento were asked to testify," Kiyo said. "We took a bus to San Francisco where the hearings were. I was glad this commission was formed. But we were only given five minutes each to testify in this huge auditorium. When I was done, I listened to the other stories. Most of these people had never talked about their internment experience before. They just broke down and cried. I was in tears listening to them, just totally wrung out."

The commission released its lengthy report in December 1982. It found there was no military justification for the incarceration of innocent people of Japanese ancestry who had not committed a crime. The report found the internment was due to prejudice, war hysteria, and failed political leadership. The commission recommended that the US government offer a public apology to those who had been incarcerated during World War II and that each of the sixty thousand survivors receive $20,000.

"Most of the Issei didn't live long enough to get either the money or the letter of apology, which meant a whole lot more to us than the money," Kiyo says. "The Issei suffered the most and lost the most, yet they received nothing." It took about ten years to locate all eligible survivors, so Kiyo and other camp survivors received their payments between 1990 and 2000. Some Nisei refused to accept the money, saying that no amount of money could compensate for the damages incarceration caused. Kiyo's children were grown by then. She accepted the money and shared it with them to help pay for their expenses.

The checks came with an official letter of apology from the president of the United States. Kiyo received hers, signed by President George H. W. Bush, in 1990. Kiyo treasures her letter from Bush. She gave copies to her children, and she has shown it to students during her presentations over the years. "Imagine that. Your country apologizing. Where else in the world would that happen? And to have a constitution that allows for redress of grievances."

"A Heart Filled to Bursting"

Tomomi and Shinji lived on their farm for the rest of their lives. Kiyo and most of her siblings stayed in the area. Kiyo's children and their many cousins often visited the farm to help out and to experience the joy of planting and harvesting crops. Kiyo's parents loved working the land with their grandchildren.

Kiyo's parents became US citizens in 1954. However, they were among many Issei who didn't live long enough to receive either the government's apology or the financial reparation for their incarceration.

One spring day in 1977, while Kiyo's mother was receiving treatment for lung cancer, Kiyo visited her at the farm. Tomomi should have been resting, but Kiyo found her working in the fields. "My heart was filled to bursting. This tiny person, who left her homeland for love of a man, who gave love totally to her nine children and everybody else in her path. . . . is even in her final days picking mustard greens for her children."

Several months later, in July 1977, Tomomi entered the hospital and fell into a coma with dozens of loving family members at her bedside. "Unexpectedly Mama lifted her head off the pillow. . . . She looked at each one of us, with longer glances toward her grandchildren. It was like a miracle, like a resurrection! 'Thank you very much,' Mama said. She fell back on her pillow and closed her eyes, never to open them again."

Shinji lived to be eighty-seven years old, working until the very end on the farm. "He wouldn't go to the doctor," Kiyo said, "even though it was obvious he was having a lot of pain. I called two of my brothers, and together we insisted he get off his tractor and keep his doctor's appointment. After an X-ray, the doctor told Shinji he was seriously ill and to stay off work for six months. However, he was back at work in his fields a few days later."

Shinji wanted to die in his vineyard, but he died in the hospital of complications related to an intestinal problem. "We were all there," Kiyo said. "It was so quick, everything happened so fast we had no time to think. My sister Kay—also a nurse—and I talked about it for a long time afterward. Why didn't he let us know how sick he was? He'd been hurting for a long time. It was a blessing that at the end he went so fast." When Shinji died in 1984, Kiyo, the eldest of her large family, became the family matriarch, a role she welcomes and takes very seriously. She and her siblings voted to sell the farm in 2008, and the new owners soon cleared the land for a housing development.

Return to Poston

Before Poston was a Japanese incarceration camp, it was an American Indian reservation with a small native population scattered across 400,000 acres (161,874 ha) of some of the most barren land in the United States. At the time, the Bureau of Indian Affairs had tried for decades to bring water from the Colorado River to the reservation, but that plan proved too costly. With the decision to incarcerate the Japanese, the head of the bureau offered the reservation as a site for an internment camp. In return, the federal government would expand roads, build a canal system, and extend electrical power—important infrastructure that the reservation lacked.

Kiyo helped plan for this monument at Poston, which commemorates both the Japanese Americans who were unjustly interned there and the four Colorado River Indian Tribes whose lands the US government took for the camp.

"Japanese internment was the justification needed for the expenditure of federal funds [to improve Indian lands]," said Dr. Michael Sosi, historian of the Colorado River Indian Tribes (CRIT). This federally recognized tribe consists of Chemehuevi, Mohave, Hopi, and Navajo Indians. "In this time of racial discrimination and hatred for the Japanese, the plan [for incarceration] was a way to displace one group of unwelcome people [Japanese] and use their hard work to build the infrastructure so another displaced group of people—American Indians—could be isolated there after the war," Sosi said.

Several years after the government closed down Poston as an internment camp, the bureau offered the shabby barracks, wired with electricity, to CRIT tribal members for forty dollars each. The site had schools, roads, athletic fields and, most important, fields of crops irrigated by water from the Colorado River, all from the work of Japanese internees. The federal government moved some of the barracks to plots of land throughout the reservation, while the rest crumbled into the desert over time.

Kiyo says, "Many previous internees wanted to forget all about Poston, even though we had reunions of former Poston inmates." Over time, what had started as reunion meetings grew into something larger. Kiyo explains, "By 1990 so many people were interested in a monument at the site that we established the Poston Memorial Monument Committee. At the time, Poston was the only internment site without a monument or a visitors' center." Kiyo and her cousin Hannah—also a former Poston internee—were cochairs of the monument committee. "We—the former internees—wanted a monument that told visitors, 'We were here, and this is what happened to us.' The camp is an educational tool, one that hopefully will continue to remind the younger generation of what occurred there," Kiyo said.

With CRIT's permission, the group built the monument on CRIT land. The group dedicated it at a ceremony in 1992 attended by several hundred people, mostly former internees and their families.

As cochair, Kiyo was present. However, two people there developed heatstroke and required emergency care. Kiyo left the presentation to accompany them to the hospital in the ambulance. "I was sorry to miss the program, but it was all set," Kiyo said, "and sick people were always my first priority."

Former internees had worked with CRIT members to build the monument to honor both the Japanese and American Indian communities. Each side of the monument tells a story of either the internment camp or the history of CRIT. An inscription says, "May it [the monument] serve as a constant reminder of our past so that Americans in the future will never again be denied their constitutional rights and may the remembrance of that experience serve to advance the evolution of the human spirit."

The National Park Service designated each of the ten detention sites as historical landmarks. Most of the actual barracks and other buildings have long since collapsed. Museums, monuments, and displays mark the sites. But a few of the buildings were reconstructed for viewing during guided tours. A museum at the site of the Topaz camp in Utah displays artifacts and photos. At Manzanar, visitors can view films, explore the site on foot, or tour the reconstructed mess hall. George Takei dedicated the Jerome-Rohwer Interpretative Museum and Visitor Center in Arkansas in 2013. Takei and his family were interned at Rohwer.

Kiyo Sato, Author

Writing always came naturally to Kiyo. She won first prize in a local writing contest for one of her stories when she was fifteen. The *Sacramento Union* newspaper published that story in the children's section, paying her twenty dollars. Many years later, when she was a nurse, she wrote articles for several nursing journals. But her writing career was just beginning. Kiyo wrote a memoir telling the story of her life and that of her family. Her memoir, published in 2007, was first titled *Dandelion through the Crack: The Sato Family Quest for the*

American Dream. New York publisher Soho Press purchased the book in 2009 and renamed it *Kiyo's Story: A Japanese-American Family's Quest for the American Dream.*

"What prompted me to write my story? I felt that people needed to know what the Issei—our parents—went through," Kiyo said. "It

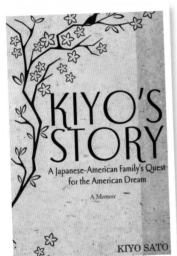

helped us come out of this experience in a positive way. Students couldn't understand why we didn't fight back or riot. It was amazing how my parents and most Issei retained their quiet dignity and didn't act like the perpetrators—the US government. The Japanese have a saying: *shikata ga nai* that means to accept what cannot be changed. That saying helped guide the Issei through the internment years."

In 2008 Stanford University librarian Michael Keller presented Kiyo with the Stanford University Libraries William Saroyan International Prize for Writing for her memoir, which is now titled *Kiyo's Story.*

It took Kiyo four years to complete her memoir, much of which she wrote while sitting in a doughnut shop near her home each morning. In 2008 the book won the Stanford University Libraries William Saroyan International Prize for Writing in nonfiction. Saroyan was an Armenian American novelist and playwright whose work won a Pulitzer Prize in 1940 and an Academy Award. Kiyo's writing prize, jointly awarded by the Stanford Libraries and the William Saroyan Foundation, is meant to encourage new and emerging writers. Not only was the award a great honor for first-time author Kiyo, but she won $12,500 in prize money.

Over the past several years, Kiyo has worked on her second book, which focuses on her lifelong love for children. "I begin by talking about our children now, what's going on in our society with abuse, homelessness, bullying, addiction, and suicide," Kiyo says. Her credentials and experience in education and nursing serve her well in this work.

"Some people insist that violence is a way of life today and we must live with it," Kiyo said. "I don't accept that. I grew up in an extremely supportive and loving family. The children always came first. Every child should have that kind of beginning. You've got to hold babies from the first moment they're born so they know the world is a safe place. Children need that baby duckling time and too many don't get it."

Continuing to Bloom

Besides writing about her life, Kiyo continues to speak publicly about her family's internment. One such event occurred in October 2018 at the Mills Station Arts and Culture Center in Rancho Cordova. Kiyo stands onstage holding a microphone. She walks across the stage once, twice, signaling the start of her presentation. Every seat is full. People stand along the walls. Children sit on the floor between rows of chairs. An elderly man enters, and a teen offers him her seat. Kiyo

Kiyo speaks about her internment experience to a packed room in October 2018 at the Mills Station Arts and Culture Center in Rancho Cordova, California.

looks around the crowded room and makes eye contact with the huge audience. Talk stops. Whispers fade to silence.

"I am Prisoner 25217-C," she begins, "a suspected spy in 1942." Some people gasp while others who know her story nod their heads. Kiyo tells her listeners that the arts center once was the Mills Station grocery store. She talks about her family's life on the farm and the day she learned her family was to be incarcerated. And she talks about life in the Poston internment camp. "It amazes me that I'm still speaking about all this more than seventy-five years later," Kiyo says. Yet she knows that many Americans still disagree about immigration and racial issues. Talking about her experience helps her audiences better understand how fear and ignorance can lead to injustice.

She stops for questions from the audience that includes teens, families, a survivor of the German concentration camps of World

War II, a Tuskegee Airman who was part of the first African American pilot squadron in World War II, and several former internees. Kiyo's voice is strong and clear. Her deep laugh is hearty, her smile warm. She interacts well with the audience, and they are very receptive to her. Two teachers in the audience ask if Kiyo will speak at their schools.

Across the room, a middle-aged man standing against a wall suddenly slumps to the floor. Someone calls 911. Meanwhile, Kiyo acts as any nurse would act. "Just hold on a minute," she says into her microphone, "and let me see what's going on." She hands the microphone to her daughter Cia

WOMAN OF THE YEAR

In 1987 two California assemblywomen founded the Woman of the Year award when they realized the California legislature had no events to mark Women's History Month in March. To celebrate the contributions by remarkable women throughout California, they invited one woman from each senate and assembly district in California to come to the state capitol in Sacramento to be honored for their accomplishments. The women were each to be recognized as Woman of the Year in a formal ceremony on the floors of the California Senate and Assembly every March.

In 2017 the California Legislative Women's Caucus awarded Kiyo Sato the California Woman of the Year award for her assembly district. Kiyo's daughter Cia was present, along with several hundred other people, to see the women receive their awards.

California assemblyman Ken Cooley, who represents much of the Sacramento district in which Kiyo lives, presented the award to her at the state capitol building in Sacramento on March 17, 2017. "Like so many Japanese Americans that were forced to leave their homes in a time of national panic and bigotry, Kiyo did not let it stop her from living an exceptionally full life," Cooley said, "She joined the Air Force, became a nurse, raised her family and is now a highly-regarded author. Kiyo has shown tremendous courage and

and tends the man until paramedics show up. The man is all right. He has fainted from the heat and crowding.

The audience remains to hear the rest of Kiyo's presentation, and she thanks them. "It's Kiyo mojo," a man calls from the audience. "We couldn't leave!" People laugh and settle down to hear what else Kiyo has to say. After the nearly two-hour presentation, Kiyo settles into a chair to sign copies of her memoir and talk with people who have questions. In less than a week, she will do a similar presentation at a church in Rocklin, California.

perseverance through her entire life and I am truly honored to see her recognized at the State Capitol for all of her extraordinary achievements." Cooley purchased copies of Kiyo's book, *Kiyo's Story*, for his entire staff.

Kiyo received the Woman of the Year award from the California state legislature in 2017. The award honors her rich life and her contributions to her community. *From left,* Assemblyman Chad Mayes, Assemblyman Ken Cooley, Kiyo, Christina Garcia (then chair of the Legislative Women's Caucus), and Assembly Speaker Anthony Rendon.

Later, reflecting on where she and her family have come since their internment, Kiyo says, "We are now nearly one hundred—my siblings, their spouses, children, grandchildren, and great-grandchildren. My siblings have been nurses, teachers, a principal, an aerospace engineer, and a soil scientist. Six of us served in the US military. We continue to bloom, inspired by the love of two immigrants who traveled to America with a dream nearly a century ago. Every new family member—whether biological or adopted—is welcomed regardless of ethnicity. We are Japanese and Caucasian; Hispanic and African American. We are Filipino and Norwegian and Irish and Chinese. And the world is a better place for it, just as Tochan predicted so long ago."

Each month since 1986, Kiyo performs with a small group of hula dancers at nursing homes, memory care homes, and VFW reunions. Hula dancing is Kiyo's favorite exercise, and she loves how patients will brighten up to sing and sway along with the dancers when they visit.

AUTHOR'S NOTE

Kiyo Sato and I met in 2015 when she attended a presentation I gave to a Northern California writing group. When the meeting ended, Kiyo and I hung back and talked. We had a lot in common. We both were nurses and published writers, and after my talk, we started going to lunch every few weeks at a café in Sacramento. Kiyo usually wore her US Air Force Nurse Corps cap or her Nisei VFW uniform and cap to our lunches. People smiled as she walked past their tables. On one occasion, a woman who had been an internee at the Granada camp in Colorado recognized Kiyo and introduced herself.

Kiyo's life story fascinated me—her childhood on a small strawberry farm, her family's incarceration in a Japanese internment camp, her nursing career, her award-winning memoir, and her years as a sought-after speaker about her internment experience. I was delighted to include a segment about her Korean War service in my 2019 book for young adult readers, *Women in the Military: From Drill Sergeants to Fighter Pilots*. I was thrilled when my editor and I agreed that Kiyo's life would be an important story for this same audience.

As part of my research, Kiyo and I regularly met at her home for more than a year. She gave me chocolate, Japanese cucumbers, and ice water with fresh lemon. I gave her flowers and books for the Little Free Library she plans to set up in her front yard. I met several of Kiyo's family members, including her sister Kay and her daughter Cia, and I interviewed nieces Jodi and Rhonda. I read dozens of articles about Kiyo's accomplishments, viewed videos in which she speaks of her internment, attended several of her public presentations, and enjoyed events marking her ninety-fifth and ninety-sixth birthdays. I also read more about the internment of Japanese Americans during World War II. Some of the most valuable resources included *I Am an American* by Jerry Stanley, *Imprisoned* by Martin W. Sandler, *Infamy* by Richard Reeves, *Un-American* by Richard Cahan and Michael Williams, and websites such as Densho, the Library of Congress, the National Archives, and Poston Preservation.

I am humbled and honored to tell the inspiring story of Kiyo Sato and her amazing family through the generations. Kiyo says telling her story to teens will help keep history alive and people will remember the injustices done to innocent Japanese immigrants and their children who were American citizens.

—Connie Goldsmith

THE SATO FAMILY

Japanese name	American name	Born	Died
Shinji (Tochan)	John	1897	1984
Tomomi (Mama)	Mary	1895	1977
Kiyo	Kiyo	1923	—
Seiji	Steve	1924	2000
Sanji	Don	1926	2005
Aizo	Ronald	1928	—
Kozo	George	1929	—
Kazu	Kay	1931	—
Naoshi	Peter	1933	—
Tomoko	Marian	1934	—
Masashi	David	1938	2008

By 1945 the Sato family—except Kiyo—used American names. Kiyo's parents selected their own names. Several of the children also picked their own names. In some cases, the children's teachers had trouble pronouncing the Japanese names and arbitrarily gave the children American names. People could pronounce "Kiyo" correctly, she said, because she was never given an American name, nor did she want one.

TIMELINE

1923	Kiyo Sato is born on a strawberry farm near Sacramento.
September 1939	World War II in Europe begins with Germany's invasion of Poland.
September 1940	Japan invades French Indochina.
September 1941	Kiyo Sato starts junior college in Sacramento.
December 1941	Japan bombs Pearl Harbor on December 7. The United States declares war on Japan the next day and enters World War II. On December 14, Japan begins its invasion of Burma.
February 1942	President Franklin D. Roosevelt signs Executive Order 9066, initiating the incarceration of nearly 120,000 Japanese Americans.
March 1942	Roosevelt signs Executive Order 9102 authorizing the creation of the War Relocation Authority to manage the transfer and incarceration of Japanese families to internment camps.
May 1942	The Sato family is taken to the temporary camp in Pinedale, California, to be held until the permanent camp was ready.
July 1942	The Sato family is taken to the permanent camp at Poston, Arizona.
October 1942	Kiyo Sato is released to attend Hillsdale College in Michigan.
May 1944	Kiyo's parents and younger siblings are released to work in Colorado.
Summer 1944	Kiyo leaves Hillsdale without graduating to be with her family in Colorado.
Fall 1944	Kiyo obtains her bachelor of science degree from Hillsdale.
December 18, 1944	The US Supreme Court justices unanimously rule in *Ex parte Mitsuye Endo v. United States* that the US government cannot continue to detain loyal American citizens. This ruling paves the way for the closing of the internment camps. In *Korematsu v. United States*, the US Supreme Court upholds the initial military justification for the internment of Japanese Americans during World War II. With the *Endo* decision, however, the justices agreed the time had come to close the camps.
January 1945	Kiyo goes alone to Sacramento to arrange for her family to move back.

May 7, 1945	Germany surrenders, bringing the war in Europe to an end.
Spring 1945	The Sato family is reunited in Sacramento.
August 6, 1945	The United States drops an atomic bomb on Hiroshima, Japan.
August 9, 1945	The United States drops an atomic bomb on Nagasaki, Japan.
September 2, 1945	Japan surrenders to the United States, and World War II ends.
Fall 1948	Kiyo graduates from Reserve Western University with a master's degree in nursing.
1951–1952	Kiyo serves in the US Air Force Nurse Corps in the Korean War.
Spring 1952	Kiyo begins work in public health and school nursing.
Fall 1952	Kiyo joins the Nisei VFW Post 8985.
1985	Kiyo retires from school nursing.
	Kiyo begins speaking to students and civic organizations around the United States about her internment experience.
2007	Kiyo's memoir *Dandelion through the Crack* (later called *Kiyo's Story*) is published and wins several writing awards.
2017	Kiyo wins the Woman of the Year award for her assembly district in Sacramento, California.
2018	Kiyo speaks to several groups about her internment experience, including her presentation at Mills Station Arts and Culture Center in Rancho Cordova, California.
2019	Kiyo visits several elementary schools to administer vision tests to the schools' youngest children.

GLOSSARY

assembly centers: temporary detention facilities that were hasty makeovers of fairgrounds, vacant fields, industrial sites, and racetracks to house Japanese Americans until the completion of permanent internment camps

Executive Order 9066: On February 19, 1942, President Roosevelt signed the executive order authorizing establishment of an Exclusion Zone in the western United States. Authorities knew the order's intent was to exclude all people of Japanese ancestry from the zone, including those who were American citizens, even though the order did not specify this.

Executive Order 9102: On March 18, 1942, President Roosevelt signed the executive order authorizing the creation of the War Relocation Authority to manage the transfer and incarceration of Japanese families to internment camps.

Executive Order 9981: On July 26, 1948, President Truman signed the executive order calling for equality of treatment and opportunity for all persons in the armed services regardless of race, color, religion, or national origin. This important first step for integration in the military did not specifically ban segregation.

Ex parte Mitsuye Endo v. United States: a US Supreme Court decision in December 1944 in which the justices unanimously ruled that the US government could not continue to detain a citizen who was loyal to the United States

Federal Bureau of Investigation (FBI): the US government agency with a goal of protecting and defending the United States and upholding and enforcing criminal laws. During World War II, the agency investigated many Japanese and Japanese Americans, searching for potential traitors and arresting those suspected of treachery.

442nd Regimental Combat Team: American Nisei men (most of whom had been incarcerated) known for especially courageous fighting in Europe during World War II. They became the most decorated unit, for the regiment's size and the men's length of service, in US military history. It incorporated the 100th Infantry Battalion in 1944, but both units kept their own designations.

Great Depression: a worldwide economic downturn (1929–1942) that was the longest and most severe economic collapse experienced by the industrialized Western world

internment camps: the ten large camps in which the US government imprisoned nearly 120,000 people of Japanese ancestry during World War II. The government claimed the internees were threats to national security, although later documentation showed they were not. The camps were sometimes called incarceration camps, and some internees called them concentration camps.

Issei: a Japanese term (pronounced ee-say) referring to the first generation of Japanese immigrants to the United States. According to US law at the time, these newcomers were not allowed to become American citizens. Beginning in 1868, Japanese immigrants moved to Hawaii and to the US mainland until the Immigration Act of 1924 cut off all immigration from Asia. Kiyo Sato's parents were Issei.

kodomo no tameni: a Japanese saying (pronounced koh-doh-moh noh tah-may-nee) that means "for the sake of the children." It expresses the philosophy that children should not bear the weight and unhappiness of adult problems.

Korematsu v. United States: a US Supreme Court decision in December 1944 upholding the military initial justification for the internment of Japanese Americans during World War II. The case was revisited in 1983, clearing Fred Korematsu of any wrongdoing.

Momotaro: a popular hero of Japanese folklore whose name means "Peach Boy"

Nisei: a Japanese term (pronounced nee-say) for the second generation of Japanese Americans born of Issei parents. Kiyo Sato and her eight siblings are Nisei. Because they were born in the United States, they are American citizens.

ofuro: a Japanese hot tub made of wood

100th Infantry Battalion: an infantry unit largely made up of Hawaiian Nisei (who had not been incarcerated). During World War II, they fought in North Africa and Italy, participating in the liberation of Rome.

reparations: making amends for a wrong by paying money to or otherwise helping those who have been wronged. In 1988 the US government officially determined that the internment of Japanese Americans during World War II had been unlawful. The government awarded survivors of the internment camps $20,000 each and a letter of apology signed by the US president.

Sansei: a Japanese term (pronounced sahn-say) for the third generation of Japanese Americans, born of Nisei parents. Kiyo Sato's nieces and nephews are Sansei.

Tochan: the Sato family word for "father," or "dad"

War Relocation Authority: the US government agency established through Executive Order 9102 to handle the forced relocation and internment of Japanese Americans during World War II

yokata ne: Japanese words (pronounced yoh-kah-tah nay) for "that's good"

SOURCE NOTES

7 John Shinji Sato, haiku, in Kiyo Sato, *Kiyo's Story: A Japanese-American Family's Quest for the American Dream* (New York: Soho, 2009), 330.

7 Sato, haiku translation by Kiyo Sato, 2019.

8 Kiyo Sato, interview with the author, July 19, 2018.

8 Sato.

9 Sato.

8–10 Sato.

11 Sato, interview, August 10, 2018.

14 Sato, *Kiyo's Story*, 36.

15 Sato, 36.

15 Sato, interview, July 12, 2018.

15 Tomomi Sato, in *Kiyo's Story*, 44.

16 James D. Phelan, "Japanese Americans during WWII: Relocation & Internment. Personal Justice Denied. Part I, Nisei and Issei," National Archives, 32, July 22, 2018, https://www.archives.gov/files/research /japanese-americans/justice-denied/chapter-1.pdf.

16 "James D. Phelan," Densho Encyclopedia, accessed August 13, 2019, http://encyclopedia.densho.org/James%20D.%20Phelan/.

17–18 Sato, *Kiyo's Story*, 41.

18 Sato, 51.

19 Sato, interview, July 17, 2018.

19 Sato, interview, July 12, 2018.

20 Sato, *Kiyo's Story*, 55.

20 Sato, 59.

21 Sato, 82.

22 Sato, interview, June 30, 2018.

22 "Speech by President Franklin D. Roosevelt, New York," transcript, Library of Congress, December 8, 1941, https:// www.loc.gov/resource/afc1986022.afc1986022_ms2201/?st=text.

23 Sato, interview, July 12, 2018.

23 "Roosevelt," Library of Congress.

25 Sato, interview, July 19, 2018.

25 Sato, *Kiyo's Story*, 90.

26 Sato, interview, July 19, 2018.

26 Sato, *Kiyo's Story*, 91.

26 Sato, 91.

26–27   Sato, interview, July 19, 2018.

28   Jerry Stanley, *I Am an American: A True Story of Japanese Internment* (New York: Crown, 1994), 17.

28   "Action on Japs," *Los Angeles Times*, February 19, 1942, A4 [available at https://www.newspapers.com/newspage/380680105/].

28   Michael Holland and John Rabe, "LA Mayor Bowron's Role in the Japanese American Internment," KPCC, February 15, 2017, https://www.scpr.org/programs/offramp/2017/02/15/55098/la-mayor-bowron-s-role-in-the-japanese-american-in/.

30   Sato, interview, August 23, 2018.

30   Sato, *Kiyo's Story*, 94.

30   Sato, 95.

30   Sato, *Kiyo's Story*, 95.

31   Sato, interview, July 19, 2018.

31   Sato, *Kiyo's Story*, 95–96.

31   Sato, 96.

32   Henry L. Stimson, quoted in "A More Perfect Union: Japanese Americans and the U.S. Constitution," Smithsonian, accessed August 16, 2019, https://amhistory.si.edu/perfectunion/non-flash/removal_crisis.html.

33   John DeWitt, quoted in "A Brief History of Japanese American Relocation during World War II," US National Park Service, accessed August 16, 2019, https://www.nps.gov/articles/historyinternment.htm.

34   Sato, interview, July 19, 2018.

34   Sato.

35   Sato.

35   Sato.

35   Sato, interview, July 27, 2018.

36   Sato.

37   Sato, *Kiyo's Story*, 112.

37   Sato, 112.

38   Sato, 115.

39   Sato, 117.

39   Sato, interview, July 27, 2018.

39–40   Sato.

40   Sato.

40   Sato, *Kiyo's Story*, 122.

40   Sato, 122–123.

41   *Power of Words Handbook: A Guide to Language about Japanese Americans in WWII*, National Japanese American Citizens League Power of

Words II Committee, April 27, 2013, https://jacl.org/wordpress/wp
-content/uploads/2015/08/Power-of-Words-Rev.-Term.-Handbook.pdf.

42   Sato, interview, July 27, 2018.

42   Sato, *Kiyo's Story*, 124.

42   Sato, 124.

43   Sato, 125.

43–44   Sato, interview, July 27, 2018.

44   Sato, *Kiyo's Story*, 127–128.

44   Yamato Ichihashi, in Richard Cahan and Michael Williams, *Un-American: The Incarceration of Japanese Americans during World War II* (Chicago: CityFiles. 2016), 116.

45   George Takei, in "8 Questions," *Time,* 194 no. 7, (August 26, 2019): 72.

45   George Takei, in Abby Ginzberg and Ken Schneider, *And Then They Came for Us* (Berkeley, CA: Films for Justice, 2017), at 18:37, https://vimeo .com/240198975.

45–46   Sato, *Kiyo's Story*, 130.

46   Sato, interview, July 27, 2018.

46   Sato.

46–47   Sato.

47   Sato, *Kiyo's Story*, 132.

47   Sato, 132–133.

48   Elizabeth Partridge, in Ginzberg and Schneider, *And Then They Came*, at 8:30.

50   Sato, *Kiyo's Story*, 134.

50   Sato, interview, July 27, 2018.

50–51   Sato.

51   Sato, interview, August 2, 2018.

52   Sato, *Kiyo's Story*, 137.

52   Sato, 137.

53   Sato, interview, August 2, 2018.

53   Sato.

53   Sato.

53–54   Sato, *Kiyo's Story*, 145.

54   Sato, interview, August 2, 2018.

54   Sato.

55   Sato.

58   Sato.

58   Sato, interview, March 14, 2019.

60 Sato, interview, August 2, 2018.

60 Sato, *Kiyo's Story*, 161.

60 Sato, 153.

62 Sato, 176.

62–63 Franklin Roosevelt, February 3, 1943, Stanford University's Hoover Institution Archives, accessed August 21, 2019, https://digitalcollections .hoover.org/savetopdf/39676/XX343.30052.

63 Sato, interview, August 2, 2018.

63 Sato.

64 Sato, interview, December 13, 2018.

64 Sato, *Kiyo's Story*, 174.

64 Sato, 179.

64 Sato, interview, February 15, 2019.

65 Sato, *Kiyo's Story*, 181.

65 Sato, interview, August 23, 2019.

66 Sato, interview, September 13, 2018.

67 Sato, *Kiyo's Story*, 183.

68 Sato, 184.

68 Sato, 184–185.

69 Sato, interview, December 13, 2018.

70 Sato, interviews, August 17, 2018, February 15, 2019.

70 Sato, interview, August 17, 2018.

70 Sato, *Kiyo's Story*, 201–202.

71 Sato, interview, March 14, 2019.

72 Sato, *Kiyo's Story*, 205.

72 Sato, 207.

72 Sato, 208.

73 Sato, interview, September 13, 2018.

74 Sato, *Kiyo's Story*, 228.

74 Sato, 228–229.

74–75 Sato, 232.

75 Sato, 233.

75 Sato, 234–235.

76 Sato, 243–244.

77–78 Sato, 237.

78 Sato, 238.

78 Sato, 239.

79 Sato, interview, December 13, 2018.

79 Sato, *Kiyo's Story*, 267.

79 Sato, 243–244.

79 Sato, 245–246.

79–80 Sato, 246–247.

80 Sato, 246–247.

81 Sato, interview, March 14, 2019.

81 Sato, *Kiyo's Story*, 250.

81 Sato, interview, March 14, 2019.

82 Sato.

82 Sato, interview, September 6, 2018.

83 Sato, interview, September 13, 2018.

83 John Sato, quoted in Sato, *Kiyo's Story*, 266.

83 Sato, 263.

83 Sato, *Kiyo's Story*, 269.

84 Justice Robert Jackson, quoted in *Facts and Case Summary—Korematsu v. U.S.*, About Federal Courts, accessed August 27, 2019, https:// www.uscourts.gov/educational-resources/educational-activities/facts -and-case-summary-korematsu-v-us.

85 Mitsuye Endo, quoted in Brian Niiya, "Mitsuye Endo: The Woman behind the Landmark Supreme Court Case," *Densho* (blog), March 24, 2016, https://densho.org/mitsuye-endo/.

86 Sato, interview, December 13, 2018.

86–87 Sato, interview, October 12, 2017.

87 Dean Della Rowe, who had received Johns Hopkins letter to Kiyo Sato, June 6, 1944.

87–88 Sato, *Kiyo's Story*, 201.

88 Sato, interview, September 13, 2018.

90 Sato, interview, October 12, 2017.

90 Sato, interview, September 20, 2018.

91 Harry S. Truman, quoted in Andrew Glass, "Truman Ends Racial Segregation in Armed Forces, July 26, 1948," Politico, accessed August 23, 2019, https://www.politico.com/story/2018/07/26/this-day-in-politics-july -26-1948-735081.

91 "Kiyo Sato-Viacrucis," Japanese American National Museum, accessed September 19, 2018, http://www.discovernikkei.org/en/resources /military/463/.

91 "Kiyo Sato-Viacrucis."

91 Sato, interview, January 9, 2019.

92 Sato, interview, October 12, 2017.

92   Sato, interview, April 4, 2019.

92   "Kiyo Sato-Viacrucis," Japanese American National Museum.

93   Sato, interview, October 12, 2017.

93   Sato, interview, April 4, 2019.

93   Sato, interview, September 20, 2018.

93   Sato, interview, April 4, 2019.

94   Sato.

95   Sato, interview, December 13, 2018.

96   Sato, interview, September 20, 2018.

96   Sato, interview, April 4, 2019.

96   Sato interview, September 20, 2018.

96   Sato.

97   Sato, interview, February 4, 2019.

97   Kiyo Sato, in "Secrets Revealed: The Presidio Project," interview, National Japanese American Historical Society, September 16, 2011, 10.

98   Jodi Sato King, interview with the author, October 28, 2018.

98–99   King.

99   Sato, interview, October 4, 2018.

99   Rhonda Sato Ransom, interview with the author, October 10, 2018.

100   Kiyo Sato, personal materials, questionnaire on "Choices of the Internment Camps" used during school presentations.

100   Kiyo Sato, personal materials, used with permission.

101   Sato, interview, August 30, 2018.

102   Sato.

102   Sato, interview, January 9, 2019.

103   Sato, *Kiyo's Story*, 317.

103   Sato, 322.

103   Sato, interview, February 15, 2019.

103   Sato.

105   Michael Sosi, in Frank Mastropolo, "An Internment Camp within an Internment Camp," *ABC News*, February 19, 2008, https://abcnews.go.com/US/story?id=4310157&page=1.

105   Sato, interview, January 25, 2019.

106   Sato, interview, March 28, 2019.

106   Mark Halverson, "Lest We Forget History," *Sacramento News and Review*, February 17, 2005, https://www.newsreview.com/sacramento/lest-we-forget-history/content?oid=33875.

107   Sato, interview, October 4, 2018.

108   Sato.

108   Sato, interview, September 20, 2018.

109   Kiyo Sato, speaking at Mills Station Arts and Culture Center, Rancho
       Cordova, CA, October 18, 2018.

110   Sato.

110–111   Ken Cooley, in "Kiyo Sato Named Woman of the Year at Annual
       Celebration," *Sacramento American River Messenger*, March 10, 2017,
       http://www.americanrivermessenger.com/articles/2017/0310-Kiyo-Sato
       -Woman-Year/index.php?ID=3198.

111   Unidentified male audience member, at Sato's Mills Station presentation.

112   Sato, interview, December 13, 2018.

SELECTED BIBLIOGRAPHY

Cahan, Richard, and Michael Williams. *Un-American: The Incarceration of Japanese Americans during World War II*. Chicago: CityFiles, 2016.

Drotar, Trina L. "Kiyo Sato Tells Story of WWII Internment." *Rancho Cordova (CA) Grapevine Independent*, November 2, 2018. http://www.ranchocordovaindependent.com/back-issues/pdf_files/vol_50_pdfs/RC%20INDEPENDENT-11-02-18.pdf.

"Kiyo Sato Named Woman of the Year at Annual Celebration." *Sacramento American River Messenger*, March 10, 2017. http://www.americanrivermessenger.com/articles/2017/0310-Kiyo-Sato-Woman-Year/index.php?ID=3198.

"Kiyo Sato-Viacrucis." Japanese American National Museum. Accessed September 19, 2018. http://www.discovernikkei.org/en/resources/military/463/.

Mastropolo, Frank. "An Internment Camp within an Internment Camp." *ABC News*, February 9, 2009. https://abcnews.go.com/US/story?id=4310157&page=1.

"The Nisei Diploma Project." *Sac City Express*, March 22, 2010. http://saccityexpress.com/the-nisei-diploma-project/.

Ownbey, Will. "A Morning with Kiyo Sato." *Sac City Express*, February 6, 2015. http://saccityexpress.com/a-morning-with-kiyo-sato/.

Power of Words Handbook: A Guide to Language about Japanese Americans in WWII. National Japanese American Citizens League Power of Words II Committee, April 27, 2013. https://jacl.org/wordpress/wp-content/uploads/2015/08/Power-of-Words-Rev.-Term.-Handbook.pdf.

Sato, Kiyo. *Kiyo's Story: A Japanese-American Family's Quest for the American Dream*. New York: Soho, 2009.

Stanley, Jerry. *I Am an American: A True Story of Japanese Internment*. New York: Crown, 1994.

Travis, Joan M. "Poston Memorial Monument the Reason It Was Built." *Parker (AZ) Pioneer*, February 24, 2014. https://www.parkerpioneer.net/news/article_43c20606-a624-5521-84f1-4ba31e0aae73.html.

FURTHER INFORMATION

Books

Goldsmith, Connie. *Bombs over Bikini: The World's First Nuclear Disaster.*
Minneapolis: Twenty-First Century Books, 2014.
Beginning in 1946, shortly after the end of World War II, the United States started an extensive nuclear bomb-testing program in the Marshall Islands of the South Pacific Ocean. Many islanders lost their ancestral home, while others experienced significant radioactive fallout, as did the crew of a Japanese fishing vessel in 1954.

Grady, Cynthia. *Write to Me: Letters from Japanese American Children to the Librarian They Left Behind.* Illustrated by Amiko Hirao. Boston: Charlesbridge, 2018.
Intended for very young readers, this charming book describes how one librarian asked her students who were to be incarcerated to write to her and share their stories. The letters are part of the Japanese American National Museum.

Hirasuna, Delphine. *The Art of Gaman: Arts and Crafts from the Japanese American Internment Camps 1942–1946.* Photography by Terry Heffernan. Berkeley, CA: Ten Speed, 2005.
Gaman is a Japanese word for endurance with grace and dignity in the face of what seems unbearable, an apt description of life in the internment camps. More than 150 examples of some of the amazing art created in wood, fabric, yarn, and other media shows the strength of the human experience.

Houston, Jeanne Wakatsuki, and James D. Houston. *Farewell to Manzanar: The Powerful True Story of Life inside a Japanese American Internment Camp.* New York: Houghton Mifflin, 1973.
Perhaps one of the best-known internment memoirs, it tells the story of a fishing family from Long Beach, California, that was incarcerated at Manzanar. The FBI arrested the author's father, leaving her mother to cope alone in the camp with her children.

Kadohata, Cynthia. *Weedflower.* New York: Atheneum Books for Young Readers, 2006.
This novel tells the story of twelve-year-old Sumiko. Raised on a California flower farm, she was interned at the Poston camp in Arizona. Sumiko befriends an Indian boy who is just as angry that the camp is on his land as she is horrified to be a prisoner there. The story offers intriguing insights into life inside the camp.

Marrin, Albert. *Uprooted: The Japanese American Experience during World War II.* New York: Alfred A. Knopf, 2016.
This nonfiction book for teens commemorates the seventy-fifth anniversary of the Japanese bombing of Pearl Harbor. It was a National Book Award finalist and a Siebert Honor book. The author focuses on the history of racism in the

United States (as well as in Japan), which contributed to President Franklin Roosevelt's decision to send an estimated 120,000 people of Japanese descent into concentration camps in WWII.

Nagai, Mariko. *Dust of Eden*. Park Ridge, IL: Albert Whitman & Company, 2018.
Told in poignant verse, this middle grade novel tells the story of thirteen-year-old Mina Masako Tagawa and her Japanese American family, who were sent from their home in Seattle to the Minidoka internment camp in Idaho in 1942.

Reeves, Richard. *Infamy: The Shocking Story of the Japanese American Internment in World War II*. New York: Picador, 2015.
This powerful book includes a discussion of politics, interviews, letters, newspapers, and archival photos, which together tell the story of internment.

Sandler, Martin W. *Imprisoned: The Betrayal of Japanese Americans during WWII*. London: Walker Books for Young Readers, 2013.
Sandler offers numerous interviews with internment camp survivors and tells of their lives before, during, and after incarceration. Some of the interviews include the heroes of the all-Nisei 442nd Regimental Combat Team in World War II and the Nisei translators whose work remained secret until the 1970s. Kiyo Sato had a brother in each of those services.

Stelson, Caren. *Sachiko: A Nagasaki Bomb Survivor's Story*. Minneapolis: Carolrhoda Books, 2016.
This award-winning book for young readers tells the true story of six-year-old Sachiko Yasui, who survived the atomic bombing of Nagasaki in 1945. Most of Sachiko's family died of radiation-related illnesses. She survived, devoting much of her later adult life to speaking about her experience of the bombing and advocating for peace, especially for children.

Takei, George, Justin Eisinger, and Steven Scott. *They Called Us Enemy*. Illustrated by Harmony Becker. Marietta, GA: Top Shelf, 2019.
George Takei (formerly an actor on television's *Star Trek* series) and his family were part of the tens of thousands of Japanese Americans incarcerated in a camp during World War II. This best-selling graphic novel tells Takei's firsthand account of his years behind barbed wire and the joys and terrors of growing up under legalized racism.

Uchida, Yoshiko. *Journey to Topaz*. New York: Scribner, 1971.
This classic novel tells of eleven-year-old Yuki and her family, sent to the internment center in Topaz, Utah. The book has been republished several times, and the latest 1984 edition includes a new prologue by the author. In the prologue, Uchida expresses her hope that young Americans will realize the injustice of the incarceration and will not permit such an event to occur again.

Organizations

Densho

https://densho.org/

The mission of this nonprofit is to preserve the testimonies of unjustly incarcerated Japanese Americans during World War II. This site offers firsthand histories of formerly incarcerated Japanese Americans, a blog, glossary, digital repository of photographs, documents, newspapers, letters, and other primary source materials about World War II incarceration. Also included is a learning center with online courses about the history of the Japanese in America and the incarceration experience. *Densho*, in Japanese, means "to pass on to future generations."

Library of Congress

https://www.loc.gov/collections/japanese-american-internment-camp-newspapers

Japanese Americans interned at assembly centers and internment camps during World War II produced Japanese American internment camp newspapers from 1942 to 1946. This collection looks into the daily lives of the people held in these camps. They include articles written in English and Japanese. They advertise community events, provide logistical information about the camps and relocation, report on community news, and include editorials.

National Archives

https://www.archives.gov/research/alic/reference/military/japanese-internment.html

Read documents and information about the incarceration of innocent Japanese and Japanese Americans in World War II. View lesson plans, archival photographs, Truman Presidential Library material relevant to the internment, and much more.

National Park Service

https://www.nps.gov/articles/japanese-american-internment-archeology.htm

Learn about the preservation of Manzanar, Minidoka, and Tule Lake camps. Numerous articles detail information about the camps and a history of incarceration during World War II. Photos include a reconstructed exhibit of a barracks room at Manzanar showing the crowded conditions in which inmates lived. The site also discusses visiting the camps, what to expect at visitor centers, and more information about displays that deepen the understanding of the internment camp experience.

Poston Preservation

https://www.postonpreservation.org

This organization's mission is to preserve some of the remaining historic structures at the internment camp at Poston, Arizona. At the visitor's center, people can hear more about the stories of Japanese Americans interned at Poston. The website contents detail the history of the camp, its post-World War II use by the Colorado River Indian Tribes, and a list of the many Nisei men who served in World War II (including Kiyo Sato's brother Sanji Sato). Maps of the camp allow viewers to locate the Sato family barracks in Poston II. A six-minute video describes the history of Poston and shows the visitor center.

Videos and Audio Recordings

"George Takei on the Japanese Internment Camps during WWII." YouTube
video, 7:00. Posted by FoundationInterviews, November 29, 2011. https://
www.youtube.com/watch?v=yogXJl9H9z0.
Activist and actor George Takei discusses his experience of being incarcerated with
his family when he was four years old and how it affected him and his parents.

Ginzberg, Abby, and Ken Schneider. *And Then They Came for Us*. Berkeley, CA: Films
for Justice, 2017. 50:00.
This documentary film is available at some libraries or for purchase online.
Comments by human rights advocate George Takei and author Elizabeth
Partridge follow the film, which describes the incarceration and compares it
to twenty-first-century discrimination and prejudice against other minorities,
such as Muslims and Latinos. Viewers can watch a trailer at https://
www.youtube.com/watch?v=I6G2yfaLNyI.

"Internment—Time of Remembrance—Kiyo Sato." YouTube video,
30:53. Posted by SECCEducationalTV, November 27, 2013. https://
www.youtube.com/watch?v=l05XWZyHO_g.
This interview with Kiyo Sato covers much of her life, including recent years.
(The film errs in naming the camp in which Kiyo was interned. She was
incarcerated at Poston in Arizona.)

"Kayo Sato Author 'Dandelion through the Crack.'" *C-Span*, interview, 17:15,
September 10, 2015. https://www.c-span.org/video/?328870-1/dandelion-crack.
This interview with Kiyo Sato is sprinkled with archival film footage and
reporting of the internment.

"Looking Like the Enemy." YouTube video, 6:59. Posted by Densho, April 9, 2015.
https://www.youtube.com/watch?v=sUEXSNBVdGY&t=323s.
This brief documentary includes the radio broadcast announcing the bombing
of Pearl Harbor, the racist headlines in newspapers, Dr. Seuss's bigoted cartoons,
and interviews with former internees.

"Manzanar: Never Again." YouTube video, 14:20. Posted by PBS, August 27, 2009.
https://www.youtube.com/watch?v=XgmY2P-xT_Y.
The documentary, narrated by Ken Burns and former internees, is about life in
the Manzanar camp.

"Momotaro, or the Story of the Son of a Peach." Audio, 23:40, from Yei Theodora
Ozaki, *Japanese Fairy Tales*. https://etc.usf.edu/lit2go/72/japanese-fairy-tales
/4845/momotaro-or-the-story-of-the-son-of-a-peach/.
Taken from a version of this traditional story, this recording covers the entire tale.

Order 9066. American Public Media and Smithsonian's National Museum of
American History. https://www.apmreports.org/order-9066.
This series of podcasts, published in 2018, features eight episodes averaging

twenty-five to thirty-five minutes each. They cover the Japanese incarceration, from the bombing of Pearl Harbor, Executive Order 9066, the internee experience, and the movement for reparations.

"President Franklin Roosevelt's 'Day of Infamy' Speech." National Archives Catalog, 11:04. https://catalog.archives.gov/id/1436350.
Hear the original radio recording of President Franklin Roosevelt's broadcast of December 8, 1941, in which he announced to the nation the Japanese bombing of the naval base at Pearl Harbor, Hawaii.

Sacramento Kings (@Sacramento Kings). "Thanks to Air Force Veteran Capt. Kiyo Sato for Being Our @Sharif Hometown Hero." Twitter, February 4, 2019, 10 p.m. https://twitter.com/SacramentoKings/status/1092664115191898112.
This short video documents the Sacramento Kings basketball team as it honors US Air Force veteran captain Kiyo Sato as its hometown hero on February 4, 2019. Kiyo's image appeared on the auditorium's giant jumbotron screen, although that segment does not appear on this short video.

"StoryCorps: Injustice Endured for the Sake of the Children." Capital Public Radio video, 4:28, December 1, 2015. http://www.capradio.org/61820.
Cia Vancil, Kiyo Sato's daughter, briefly interviews her mother about her internment.

"StoryCorps: Kiyo Sato, Cia Vancil." YouTube video, 50:06. Posted by the Sacramento Public Library, September 3, 2016. https://www.youtube .com/watch?v=SGBEQInHKFQ.
Cia Vancil interviews her mother about her experience at the Poston internment camp after the bombing of Pearl Harbor.

INDEX

Adams, Ansel, 48, 59
agriculture, 19, 71
   farming, 46
assembly centers, 36, 41,
   84, 117
   See also temporary
   detention centers
atomic bomb, 88, 116
   Hiroshima, Japan,
   88–89, 116
   Nagasaki, Japan,
   88–89, 116

Baptist, 21, 31, 63
Beskeen, John, 26, 27,
   75, 78
Blackbird Vision
   Screening System, 93
Bowron, Fletcher, 28
Bureau of Indian Affairs,
   104, 105
Bush, George H. W.,
   101–102

California, 4, 16–20,
   28, 31–32, 44, 51,
   56, 59, 74, 77, 85,
   94–97, 109–111
   Barstow, 52
   Fresno, 37, 42, 50, 56
   Napa Valley, 11, 13
   Sacramento, 8, 11,
   14, 17, 18, 21, 24,
   61–62, 66, 68, 71,
   73–75, 78, 80–82,
   86, 88, 90, 93–95,
   98, 101, 110, 113
   San Francisco, 11–13,
   16, 22, 32–34,
   44–45, 49, 84–85,
   97, 101
   San Leandro, 84

California Civil Liberties
   Public Education
   Fund, 99
Citizen Isolation Centers,
   57
Civil Control Station, 31
Commission on Wartime
   Relocation and
   Internment of
   Civilians, 101, 102
Cooley, Ken, 110–111
Cox, Mary Aline, 19, 27,
   39, 66, 67, 78

*Dandelion through the
   Crack: The Sato
   Family Quest for the
   American Dream*,
   106, 107, 116.
   See also *Kiyo's Story:
   A Japanese-American
   Family's Quest for the
   American Dream*
Department of Justice
   Internment Camps,
   56
DeWitt, John L., 33–34
Dr. Seuss (Theodor Seuss
   Geisel) 28,29

Education
   Edward Kelley School,
   19, 21, 27, 66, 78,
   81
   Frances Payne Bolton
   School of Nursing,
   87, 89
   Hillsdale College,
   63–65, 67, 68–71,
   73, 86, 115
   Kit Carson Junior
   High, 21, 81

Sacramento High
   School, 81
Western Reserve
   University (Case
   Western Reserve
   University), 87, 116
Western State Teacher's
   College (Western
   State Colorado
   University), 73
Eisenhower, Milton, 63
Embree, Catherine, 64
emigration, 16
English language, 15, 59
Exclusion Zone, 32, 34,
   63, 117. *See also*
   Executive Orders
Executive Orders, 33
   9066, 32–33, 62, 101,
   115, 117
   9102, 32, 115, 117–118
   (*see also* War Relocation
   Authority)
   9981, 91, 117

Fairbairn, Marjorie, 21,
   39
Federal Bureau of
   Investigation (FBI),
   30, 31, 56, 68–69,
   84, 117
forced removal, 41, 49
442nd Regimental
   Combat Team, 117

Geisel, Theodor Seuss,
   28, 29
Great Depression, 20,
   48, 117
group toilets, 45, 46, 55

Haberstitch, David, 66

Ichihashi, Yamato, 44
Immigration Act of 1924,
    12, 118
incarceration/internment,
    4–5, 20, 32–33, 41,
    44, 66, 80, 84–85,
    94, 97–99, 101–102,
    105, 113, 115–116,
    118
incarceration/internment
    camps, 4, 9, 10,
    32, 34, 36, 41,
    43, 48–49, 51, 54,
    56–57, 62–64, 69,
    70, 77–78, 80, 83,
    85–86, 90, 99–100,
    104–106, 113, 115,
    117. See also Pinedale
    detention center;
    See also Poston
    internment camp
Manzanar internment
    camp, 48, 57, 59,
    106
Pinedale detention
    center, 37, 40, 42,
    44, 46, 50, 54–56,
    115
Poston internment
    camp, 4, 50–52,
    54–58, 60–62,
    64–66, 68–69,
    71–72, 75, 86, 104,
    109, 113
Santa Anita Park, 37,
    44, 45, 56
Tanforan Racetrack,
    44, 45, 84
Inouye, Daniel, 100
internees, 39, 42, 44, 46,
    48–49, 51, 54–55,
    58–60, 64, 69, 71,
    76, 105–106, 110,
    113, 117

Japan, 4, 10–14, 16,
    22–23, 24–26,
    30–31, 52, 82,
    87–92, 94, 115
Japanese Americans, 4, 9,
    12, 19, 20, 27–28,
    32, 33, 34, 37, 41,
    43, 48, 49, 51, 52,
    56–57, 60, 62, 71,
    75, 77, 84–85, 90,
    98, 99, 101, 104, 110,
    113, 115, 117, 118
Japanese terms
    baishakunin, 12
    hakujin, 26
    Issei, 4–5, 14, 16, 30,
        45, 56, 59, 102, 107,
        118
    kodomo no tameni, 40,
        118
    Nisei, 4–5, 16, 26–27,
        29–30, 39, 52–53,
        59, 62–64, 94–95,
        99, 102, 117–118
    Sansei, 5–6, 118
    shikata ga nai, 107
    yokatta ne, 54, 64

Keenesburg, CO, 71–72,
    74, 80
Kiyo's Story: A
    Japanese-American
    Family's Quest for the
    American Dream, 5,
    107, 111, 116
Korean War, 90, 94–95,
    100, 113, 116, 136
Korematsu v. United
    States, 115

Lange, Dorothea, 20,
    48–49
Lansing, MI, 63
Los Angeles Times, 28

McCloy, John J., 62
McDonnell family, the,
    78, 79–81
Mills Station Arts and
    Culture Center,
    108–109, 116
Mills Station grocery
    store, 26, 75, 78, 81
Momotaro, 46–47, 118

National Japanese
    American Historical
    Society, 97
Nicholsons family, 66, 67
Nisei VFW Post 8985,
    94–95
Nisei VFW Post 8986, 99
Nisei VFW Post 8987,
    113
Nisei VFW Post 8988,
    116

100th Infantry Battalion,
    62, 117

Pearl Harbor, 4, 17,
    22–27, 30, 32, 90,
    115
Phelan, James D., 16
Poston Memorial
    Monument
    Committee, 105
prisoners, 4, 41–42, 51,
    56–58, 60, 109.
    See also internees

reparations, 100–101,
    102, 118
Roosevelt, Franklin D.,
    22, 23, 32–33, 62,
    79, 115, 117

Sacramento Union, 106
San Francisco Examiner,
    28

Sato family
  Aizo (Ronald), 4, 12, 15, 51, 94, 114
  Cia, 96, 110, 113
  Hannah, 92, 105
  Jodi, 6, 98–99, 113
  Kazu (Kay), 4, 51, 54, 103, 113, 114
  Kozo (George), 4, 6, 12, 51, 81, 91–92, 94, 95, 98
  Masashi (David), 4, 12, 22, 34–35, 39, 51, 72, 81, 99
  Naoshi (Peter), 4, 12, 51, 95
  Rhonda, 99, 113
  Sanji (Don), 4, 12, 15, 42, 68–69, 70–71, 82, 94
  Seiji (Steve), 4–5, 11–12, 15, 19, 27, 51, 70, 74, 94, 95
  Shinji/Tochan (John), 4, 6, 8–9, 11–16, 17–18, 19, 20, 21–22, 25, 27, 30–31, 34–35, 37–39, 42, 46, 51, 53, 55, 58, 59, 61, 63, 67–68, 71–74, 76, 80–83, 92, 102–103, 112
  Tomoko (Marian), 4, 12, 51
  Tomomi/Mama (Mary), 4, 6, 8, 9, 10, 11–14, 15, 16, 18–22, 27–28, 30–31, 34–35, 37–40, 42–43, 51, 52–54, 64, 72–74, 77, 80–83, 102–103
Sosi, Michael, 105
Stanford University Libraries William Saroyan International Prize for Writing in nonfiction, 107, 108
Stanley, Jerry, 28, 113
Stimson, Henry L., 32
Studarus, John, 26

Takei, George, 44, 56, 106
temporary detention centers, 37, 42, 43–44, 45, 48–49, 56
  See also assembly centers
Truman, Harry, 91, 117

US Air Force, 88, 90, 91, 92, 93, 95, 110

Nurse Corps, 113, 116, 136
US Army, 4, 5, 11, 27, 28, 44, 51, 56, 71, 72, 85
US Supreme Court, 33, 84–85, 88, 115, 117–118
US Supreme Court cases
  Ex parte Mitsuye Endo v. United States, 85, 115, 117
  Korematsu v. United States, 84, 118

Viacrucis, Gene, 96

War Relocation Authority, 32, 48, 57, 63, 69, 115, 117–118
Wartime Civil Control Administration, 44
Woman of the Year award, 110, 111, 116
World War II, 4, 8, 22–23, 36, 41, 47, 56, 84, 88, 90, 94, 98, 100, 102, 110, 113, 115–118.
  See also Pearl Harbor

PHOTO ACKNOWLEDGMENTS

Image credits: Photos courtesy Kiyo Sato, pp. 9, 12, 13, 51, 68, 69, 87, 101; Wikimedia Commons (public domain), pp. 10, 29, 47; Fotosearch/Archive Photos/Getty Images, p. 17; Laura Westlund/Independent Picture Service, pp. 18, 57, 89; National Archives, pp. 20, 24, 27, 33, 37, 45, 49, 55, 85, 88; Bettmann/Getty Images, p. 23; Library of Congress, pp. 43, 59, 71; New Westminster Museum and Archives IFP0818-146, p. 66; Gerald Lamboley Collection of Japanese-American Letters, Archives Center, National Museum of American History, Smithsonian Institution, p. 67; Rebedwards/ Wikimedia Commons (CC BY-SA 4.0), p. 77; Fred T. Korematsu, Unidentified Artist, 1939 Gelatin silver print, National Portrait Gallery, Smithsonian Institution, gift of the Fred T. Korematsu Family, p. 84; Center for Sacramento History, Sacramento Bee Photographer's Negatives, Shuman 1976-10-26 Hearing Test 4a, p. 94; Courtesy Lisa Sato, p. 95; © Lizette Young, p. 98; Steven Jarrett Bernstein/Wikimedia Commons (CC BY-SA 3.0), p. 104; Independent Picture Service, p. 107 (top); Linda A. Cicero/ Stanford News Service, p. 107 (bottom); © Rick Sloan, p. 109; Courtesy California Assemblyman Ken Cooley's Office, p. 111; © Roy T. Vogel, p. 112. Design elements: Terriana/iStock/Getty Images (birds); yotrak/iStock/Getty Images, p. 1 (paper texture); sergio34/iStock/Getty Images, p. 17 (black grainy texture).

Cover: Photos courtesy Kiyo Sato.

ABOUT THE AUTHORS

Connie Goldsmith has written twenty-five nonfiction books. Her books are for young adult and middle-grade readers and deal with health topics, history, and military themes. She has also published more than two hundred magazine articles for adults and children. Her books include *Women in the Military: From Drill Sergeants to Fighter Pilots*; *Pandemic: How Climate, the Environment, and Superbugs Increase the Risk*; *Animals Go to War: From Dogs to Dolphins*; *Dogs at War: Military Canine Heroes*; *The Ebola Epidemic: The Fight, The Future* (a Junior Library Guild selection); and *Bombs over Bikini: The World's First Nuclear Disaster* (a Junior Library Guild Selection, a Children's Book Committee at Bank Street College Best Children's Book of the Year, and an SCBWI Crystal Kite winner). Goldsmith is a member of the Society of Children's Book Writers and Illustrators and the Authors Guild. She is a registered nurse with a bachelor of science degree in nursing and a master of public administration degree in health care. She lives near Sacramento, California.

Kiyo Sato was incarcerated at Poston Camp in Arizona with her family in 1942 when she was nineteen. She was released from camp early to attend college in the Midwest. Ultimately, she obtained a bachelor of science degree and a master's degree in nursing and served with the US Air Force Nurse Corps during the Korean War. Sato worked for many years in the Sacramento area as a public health and school nurse. She wrote an award-winning memoir of her life, published in 2007 as *Dandelion through the Crack*, which another publisher acquired and republished in 2009 as *Kiyo's Story: A Japanese-American Family's Quest for the American Dream*. Over the past decades, Sato has spoken to tens of thousands of young people and to civic groups about the internment experience in the hopes of preventing such an unjust event from ever occurring again. She lives near Sacramento.